God in the Marketplace is a powerful book. Henry and Richard share their wisdom on how the businessman can select the path to more Christlikeness in the marketplace.

David Cavan
President
Cavan Real Estate Investments

Many Christian executives struggle with the position their faith should occupy in their business pursuits and endeavors. This book examines this phenomenon, presenting clear, biblical perspectives on how to honor God in the marketplace—from practicing everyday disciplines to cultivating integrity and handling universal challenges to achieve his mission. This is a "must-read" for those seeking to achieve personal and business accomplishment as well as spiritual growth.

David "Mac" McQuiston
President and CEO
CEO Forum Inc.

When we discover that God is very involved in the marketplace, that he has a will and purpose, even in business, it changes our business life. This book clearly addresses all these issues. I wish I had read it about forty years ago.

Wes Cantrell
Former Chairman and CEO
Lanier Worldwide, Inc.
Coauthor, *High Performance Ethics*

You'll want a pen handy when you read *God in the Marketplace!* While friendly and approachable, each page challenges conventional wisdom with time-tested truth that you can apply tomorrow morning at work. The authors are deeply loved and widely respected among Christian business leaders. I've been honored to know them for well over a decade, and have drawn deeply from their gracious spirits and tremendous insights.

John D. Beckett
Chairman, R. W. Beckett Corporation
Author, *Loving Monday* and *Mastering Monday*

Wonderful biblical insights . . . full of stories with practical application that will have you laughing and crying.

Leo Wells III
President and Founder
Wells Real Estate Fund

As a Christian and one who has been in the corporate world for the past forty years in various positions of leadership, I can attest that Henry and Richard Blackaby's answers are relevant, helpful, instructive, and encouraging. They serve as an excellent teaching guide for any Christian in the workplace.

Ron F. Wagley
Former Chairman, CEO, and President
Transamerica Occidental Life Insurance Company

HENRY & RICHARD
BLACKABY

45 Questions
FORTUNE 500
Executives Ask
About Faith, Life,
& Business

GOD IN THE
MARKET
PLACE

FROM THE AUTHORS OF THE #1 BESTSELLER
EXPERIENCING GOD AND *SPIRITUAL LEADERSHIP*

NASHVILLE, TENNESSEE

GOD IN THE MARKETPLACE
Copyright © 2008 by Henry Blackaby and Richard Blackaby
All Rights Reserved

ISBN: 978-0-8054-4688-3
B & H Publishing Group
Nashville, Tennessee
www.BHPublishingGroup.com

Dewey Decimal Classification: 248.4
Christian Life / Work / God—Will

Printed in the USA
1 2 3 4 5 12 11 10 09 08

DEDICATION

We would like to dedicate this book to:

Gerald Richard Blackaby and Melvin A. Wells,
godly businessmen who greatly impacted
their world and our lives for God.

We would also like to thank Mac McQuiston,
president of CEO Forum, for his tireless work
among Christian CEOs. It has been our privilege
to be associated with him and to work with him.

CONTENTS

Part Three: My Devotional Life

Part Four: My Family Life

Part Five: My Church and Community Life

Part Six: My Kingdom Life

Marketplace Perspectives

PREFACE

Questions, just like people, come in all sizes and shapes. There are big questions, trivial questions, brilliant questions, foolish questions, multiple-choice questions, and questions without answers. But knowing what to ask can be as important as recognizing the answer. This book is our response to questions we have frequently been asked over the years by sincere Christians seeking to live their lives in a God-honoring manner.

Christian men and women who hold influential positions in the marketplace want to know how their relationship with God practically affects their careers and their personal lives. We work with 165 Christian CEOs of Fortune 100 and 500 companies. Henry leads a monthly Bible study, "God in the Workplace." Richard writes a monthly electronic devotional for businesspeople. We have led numerous conferences for leaders and other businesspeople. In 2001 we wrote the book *Spiritual Leadership: Moving People on to God's Agenda,* and in 2005 we authored *Called to Be God's Leader: Lessons from the Life of Joshua, How God Prepares His Servants for Spiritual Leadership.* We are gratified that God has used these books to inspire people to function as spiritual leaders where he has placed them. The books have led to numerous invitations for us to speak on spiritual leadership, not just in America but internationally, to business, government, military, and church leaders. This has been a humbling and challenging assignment, but we both strongly believe God is seeking to work mightily through those people in the business world who are wholly committed to him (2 Chron. 16:9).

Christian businesspeople who live in pressure cookers want their lives to affect more than their corporate shareholders. They want to hear what God says about leading their families. They want to use their business skills to strengthen their churches.

This book evolved from our experience as church and ministry leaders. Increasingly, Christian business leaders who know more than we'll ever hope to understand about politics, the economy, law, military, or medicine have sought us out on spiritual matters. These outstanding men and women want to understand how God uses people like them to impact his kingdom. They want to explore how the Holy Spirit's presence within them can affect how they lead their companies and their families.

God has systematically steered us toward the business community. We speak at leadership conferences all over North America and around the world endeavoring to help people develop into spiritual leaders. Christians, whether they are in government service, the military, or the marketplace, recognize that this is a critical time in world history. They want to hear clearly from God and to impact his kingdom. We have spent many hours helping businesspeople find God's direction for their lives.

As they shared their concerns, we observed a pattern of several reoccurring questions. So we decided to poll Christian CEOs from many of America's largest companies to discover the most pressing issues Christian businesspeople face. Their responses determined the topics addressed in this book.

The deepest concerns, as expressed by business leaders, fall into six general categories:

- Personal life
- Family life
- Business life
- Devotional life
- Church life
- Community and kingdom life

As you read this book, be prepared for God to speak to you. Knowing what he intends for your life will revolutionize the way you approach your business. Learning to see God's activity in your workplace will help you view the corporate office as a mission field rather than a minefield. We believe God wants to bring revival to his people, and we sense that God is strategically preparing businesspeople to be a catalyst for this to happen. It is crucial and timely that businesspeople understand their role, first and foremost, as servants of God. One's career is foundational for a greater reality—the mighty work God wants to do in and through each believer's life.

We pray this book will do much more than merely present knowledge. We hope God will use it to sensitize your heart so you can experience the amazing dimensions of his power working through your life.

Suggestions for Studying This Book

The Material

This book can be studied individually. However, discussing this material with others in a group setting is the best way to stimulate your thinking and to bring a level of accountability as you respond to what God says.

Additional Study

This book is not an exhaustive treatise of definitive answers. It is meant to begin a process through which businesspeople can find God's direction in his Word. At the end of each discussion is a section entitled "Additional Resources." Related Scripture verses are provided there. Perhaps the questions addressed will spur you to do additional study on what God's Word says on the subject.

Also cited are titles of other books that address the topic. This is by no means an exhaustive bibliography, nor does it indicate we agree with or advocate everything found in these books. But we do want to encourage you to make a serious study of these issues.

We cannot definitively answer all your questions, but through this book we want to bring you face to face with the One who can. Expect God to speak to you as you read and seek his wisdom.

INTRODUCTION

Questions
Focus Your Life

Have you ever heard of the man named Joe Outhouse? He grew so weary of the teasing over his name that he finally had it changed—to Bill Outhouse. When asked why the change to "Bill," he replied, "I was tired of my friends always saying, 'Hello, Joe, what do you know?'"

Henry's seminary professor, Dr. Gaines Dobbins, often declared, "If you ask the wrong question, you'll get the wrong answer." Some people spend an inordinate amount of time addressing irrelevant issues while neglecting matters with eternal ramifications.

We all spend much of our lives looking for answers. Millions of people around the world are motivated daily by the need to know where to obtain food for that day. Countless men and women are absorbed with how to get ahead in life. Grieving people desperately try to comprehend their loss. Most of us are in a continuing quest to discern what meaning our life has amid the billions of people populating the earth. Life is riddled with questions from the mundane to the ethereal. It's crucial, though, that Christians not waste time fretting over the trivial while neglecting the essential.

First Timothy 6:7 claims, "For we brought nothing into the world, and we can take nothing out." Scripture exhorts us, above all other goals, to pursue godliness. The benefits of holy living affect this life as well as eternity. But with so many pressing issues bombarding people today, sanctification is often not the top priority.

When we were pastors, we liked to visit people from our congregation at their job sites. We wanted to know what their life outside of church was like. One day, Richard drove downtown to visit Mike, a faithful, soft-spoken church member. He taught children's Sunday school and took a regular shift in the nursery. Mike was an easygoing, amiable guy who usually came to church dressed casually.

Mike's work address was a grand, impressive building. The receptionist was all business as she notified Mike that someone was there to see him. She led Richard through the plush executive office suite to the door of the vice president. Mike greeted Richard warmly and welcomed him into his spacious, luxurious office. Enormous windows commanded an impressive view. There was a fireplace and a Jacuzzi tub in the *en suite* bathroom. A door connected Mike's office directly with that of the owner and president.

As they visited over lunch, Mike shared some of the daily challenges he faced working closely with a non-Christian, Type A, and exceedingly ambitious boss. Mike had been required to invest a large portion of his income back into the company. He was also called on to go on business trips and to participate in various social functions which regularly tested his personal convictions. Richard now saw Mike in an entirely new light. He was not just a "regular guy" in jeans playing with toddlers on the floor of the church nursery. He was a top executive for a burgeoning company, undergoing daily pressure to compromise his Christian principles.

Mike, of course, is one of thousands of Christians whose jobs challenge their commitment to live out their faith. We have talked with numerous men and women who work in similar situations. They want their lives to honor God, but their reality includes complex job situations and ongoing, pervasive temptations to set aside their values. Sincere Christians seeking to follow God's will in the midst of a secular workplace inevitably have many questions. The following chapters will specifically address several of the most pertinent issues that Christian businesspeople tell us they face daily.

Obviously, one little book cannot answer all your questions, but as you grapple with the difficult spiritual issues that permeate the marketplace, the following suggestions may help you find answers for your specific situation.

Remember That You Belong to God

If you are a Christian, the Holy Spirit dwells within you (John 14:16–18), so Almighty God himself resides in your life. Heavenly resources, including God's wisdom, are available to you (James 1:5). Jesus said the Holy Spirit, which he called the "Spirit of truth" (John 16:13), would guide believers into all truth. The Holy Spirit knows the mind of the heavenly Father; therefore he can direct you into God's perfect will (1 Cor. 2:9–16).

Understand That God's Ways Are Not Your Ways

You are not God. His ways are above human reasoning, so they will sometimes contradict your own thinking (Isa. 55:8–9). Just because a trend or idea is considered a smart business practice or is promoted in popular leadership literature does not assure its acceptability to God. Don't superimpose your own thinking over the Bible's wisdom. Be alert because God may want to completely reorient your thinking to align it with his purposes.

Cultivate a Teachable Heart

Leaders are more accustomed to teaching others than to receiving instruction. "The one who follows instruction is on the path to life, but the one who rejects correction goes astray," says Proverbs 10:17. You can read a book every day or memorize entire volumes of Scripture, but if you lack a teachable spirit, your efforts are futile (Prov. 22:17). It is not the quantity of information you take in or how intensely you study that matters. Rather, the manner in which you accept instruction determines how your life will be changed.

Test Everything

Christian books like this one can be helpful, but they do not have the authority of the Bible (2 Tim. 3:16). Likewise, God will speak through other Christians, but they are not the final authority either. Test everything you read and hear against the timeless, authoritative Word of God. Keep your Bible close at hand when you read a book or listen to a message. Just because an author or speaker cites a Scripture verse does not guarantee the point is biblical. Scripture is often subtly and sometimes blatantly misused. Don't allow anyone else to do your thinking for you. Rather, ask the Holy Spirit to help you discern the truth God wants to teach you. If you are vigilant about using the Bible as the plumb line by which you measure everything else, it will protect you from false teaching. The more time you spend in the Word, the better you will know how to think biblically.

Be Prepared to Respond

Jesus said that when you encounter truth, it will set you free (John 8:32). You are too busy and life is too challenging for you to read the

Bible merely for head knowledge. As you read, expect God to speak to you and to change your life. And when he does, be ready immediately to obey what he has said. God is not satisfied that we know and believe what he says; he expects us to *do* what he tells us (Matt. 21:28–31; Luke 6:46; John 15:14).

Invest Your Life in Others

When you sense that God has revealed truth to you, share it with godly friends and church members to see if they concur with your understanding. Scripture strongly encourages us to seek others' counsel (Prov. 11:14). When we live our Christian life without the caution and instruction of trusted counselors, we invite disaster. If God has spoken to you, you should find that truth verified by wise believers. Bible studies or book studies like this one can be helpful, too, especially when believers collectively pool their insights and discern together what God is saying to them.

With the foundation now set, you will find a number of important questions and issues to deal with in the following chapters.

PART 1

My Personal Life

Over the years we make many choices. The results accumulate and come back to us as blessings or consequences. In Paul's words, we reap what we sow (Gal. 6:7). Our lives reflect the countless decisions we have made thus far.

You may be responsible for many employees. You may hold other leadership positions, as a parent, in your church, or as a board member. If you are a leader, you've no doubt discovered there is only one person you can truly change, and that is you. Even powerful corporate CEOs cannot fundamentally alter their employees' ethics or values; but they can, with the Holy Spirit's enabling, alter their own attitudes. So, before looking at ways to impact your family or workplace or church for God, let's begin by seeing how God wants to transform you.

History is riddled with examples of people who, because they could not master themselves, failed miserably in business as well. In 1874, Sam Andrews had a falling out with his business partner, John Rockefeller. Andrews resented Rockefeller's policy of reinvesting much of Standard Oil's profits back into the company rather than paying large dividends to stockholders. Andrews finally exclaimed, "I wish I was out of this business." Rockefeller asked his price for his shares, and Andrews demanded one million dollars. Rockefeller paid it the next day. Andrews bragged he had bested Rockefeller in business and began to spend his newly acquired fortune.

To Andrews' consternation, Rockefeller immediately sold those same shares for 1.3 million dollars to William Vanderbilt. Andrews vehemently complained that he had been cheated, so Rockefeller magnanimously offered to resell the shares to Andrews for the original price. But Andrews, his pride injured, refused the offer. Instead he proceeded to build an ostentatious mansion from which he vilified Rockefeller for the remainder of his life.

Historians have estimated that, had Andrews held on to his shares, they would have been worth over 900 million dollars by the early 1930s, making him one of America's wealthiest men. One biographer concluded: "This rash decision, motivated by pure pique and a bruised ego, kept him from becoming one of America's richest men." Andrews could not suppress his greed or his ego, so he ended up jealously on the sidelines watching others grow enormously wealthy.

With a myriad of pressures and temptations assailing them, business leaders must closely guard their personal lives and take genuine responsibility for their actions and attitudes. This chapter will address some of the most common questions we receive relating to personal issues.

What is God's ultimate goal for my life as a businessperson?

One of the best descriptions of what God intends for your life is found in Romans 8:28–30: "We know that all things work together for the good of those who love God: those who are called according to His purpose. For those He foreknew He also predestined to be conformed to the image of His Son, so that He would be the firstborn among many brothers. And those He predestined, He also called; and those He called, He also justified; and those He justified, He also glorified."

God knew you before time began. Long before you were aware of him, he understood every detail of your life (Ps. 139:13–16). Before your birth he already planned for you to become like his Son Jesus. Pause and consider the amazing ramifications of that truth. Jesus is the heavenly Father's prototype. Whenever the Father looks at you, he has Christ's image before him as the model of what he will eventually make you to become like.

People often misinterpret Romans 8:28. Consider the Christian businesswoman who boldly took a moral stand and refused to compromise her integrity to make a large sale. She was subsequently fired for not being a team player. Several of her Christian friends quoted Romans 8:28 to her and assured her with the promise, "We know God works *all* things together for good. He probably allowed you to be unjustly fired because he has a better job for you around the corner! When you get that lucrative new position, you'll be glad all this happened!"

These sincere, misguided words miss the point. Does this Scripture say we will ultimately end up enjoying comfort, respect, and prosperity when God has finished his work in our lives? Perhaps yes. Perhaps no. Actually, the greatest good God can do for us is to make us like his Son. God's primary concern for us is not our position on the corporate ladder, our retirement benefits, or our comfort. His ultimate goal for us is Christlikeness. He will allow whatever is necessary into our lives so we become like Jesus.

What circumstances and life events have made you like Christ? Have they been easy or difficult? Have God's blessings made you more Christlike than the trials you have experienced? Generally, people affirm that hard times have helped them grow the most spiritually. If this is so, then it is understandable why God allows pain in our lives (James 1:2–4). Wouldn't it be great if every time God blessed us we became more humble or holy? Wouldn't it be wonderful if, when we received a bonus, we immediately became more fervent in our prayer life? But that generally doesn't happen. More often, a financial crisis or criticism or betrayal is what drives us to humility and prayer.

So what does Romans 8:28 promise? Regardless of how arduous your circumstances, if you trust God, he will see that you come out of your situation more like Christ. You may not have the same income level as before. Your health may not be as good. You may miss some of the professional perks you previously enjoyed. But you will be more like Jesus.

Isn't it ironic that we often pray for God to make us Christlike, but the moment God allows something into our lives that would answer this prayer, we immediately send out a fervent prayer request to all our friends to have that circumstance removed? We must decide what is most important to us: comfort or Christlikeness. The process of becoming like Christ is generally not easy or comfortable, but it is the greatest thing we can ask God to do for us.

Christian businesspeople tell us many stories of suffering—times when they refused to compromise their integrity in their workplace. Some were demoted. Others lost their jobs. Even honest Christians have suffered financial loss. Many have been ostracized personally and professionally.

God, however, has done an awesome work in their lives! They are walking more closely with him than ever before. Some have led others to faith in Christ as a result of their arduous pilgrimage. Others are enjoying revitalized marriages and families because the crisis helped them reorder their priorities. Some Christians who were released from their jobs have begun ministries that are now having a global impact meeting peoples' needs. Those who have trusted God throughout the painful process have experienced the abiding joy of embracing the character traits of Jesus.

Are you undergoing an onerous circumstance? Could it be that, rather than abandoning you as you may have thought, God is actually refining you to be more like his Son?

God expects us to honor him with all of our actions (1 Cor. 10:31; 2 Cor. 5:14–15, 20). We tend to compartmentalize our lives; we have our business life, our personal life, our religious life, and so on. God does not see things that way (Ps. 139). God is equally entitled to receive honor from us whether we're teaching a Bible study, attending a board meeting, making a sales presentation, embarking on a business trip, or relating to our family. God's name is lifted up when we glorify him through adversity. Jesus said he would *never* leave us! *Every* activity in which we engage should glorify God.

Questions for Reflection

1. What are your top priorities? What do you think matters most to God?
2. How is your life presently glorifying God?
3. What attitude adjustments would help the way you view suffering and its outcome?
4. Are you currently engaging in any activity that dishonors God? If so, what alterations do you intend to make?

Additional Resources

Deuteronomy 30:11–20
Proverbs 24:17
Matthew 5–7
1 Corinthians 13
2 Corinthians 3:18
Galatians 5:22–25

Henry Blackaby and Norman Blackaby, *Called and Accountable* (Birmingham, AL: New Hope Publishers, 2005).
Henry Blackaby and Richard Blackaby, *Called to Be God's Leader: Lessons from the Life of Joshua* (Nashville: Thomas Nelson, 2004).
Henry Blackaby and Thomas Blackaby, *The Man God Uses* (Nashville: Broadman and Holman, 1999).

How should I model Christ to the people I work with?

Christian character is not something you have to work up or put on. It's the natural result of the Holy Spirit's activity in a believer's life (Gal. 5:22–23). Christian character is Christ expressing his life through you (1 Cor. 15:10; Gal. 2:20). It comes from abiding in Christ (John 15:5, 7–8). What your boss and staff see each day is the result of your time walking with God (Luke 3:4–6; Acts 4:13).

John 17 offers powerful insight into how Jesus dealt with those over him and those under him. His Father had given him a specific assignment, entrusting to him twelve men through whom he would extend the good news of salvation around the world (John 17:6). Jesus had walked with these disciples for an extended period of time, and now he was giving an account to his Father.

While the entire chapter is filled with rich insights into Jesus' prayer life, notice two verses primarily. In John 17:1, Jesus prayed: "Father . . . glorify Your Son so that the Son may glorify You." It might appear unusual, even self-centered and inappropriate to ask God to glorify *us*. Yet this is what Jesus prayed.

The word *glorify* means to exalt, magnify, or lift up. When we glorify God, we hold up his character and nature so the world can see what he is like. Jesus prayed that the Father would lift *him* up so the watching world could see the heavenly Father's character. It was as if Jesus was asking his Father to put a magnifying glass over his life so people could take a close look. When people scrutinized Jesus' life, he wanted them to come away impressed with his Father (Luke 9:43). And they did!

Could you pray that prayer? "Heavenly Father, would you put *my* life in a place where people could observe my conduct as a Christian businessperson and marvel at you?" When people see you forgive those who mistreat you, they should conclude that your God is a forgiving God. When they experience your patience, kindness, and generosity, their favorable impression of your conduct should be a reflection of your God.

A second verse that may challenge you is John 17:19: "I sanctify Myself for them, so they also may be sanctified by the truth." A Christian leader, parent, teacher, employer, or politician has an increased accountability to God (James 3:1). Their actions affect not only themselves but also those under their influence. When they live carelessly, they create stumbling blocks for others who are trying to walk with God (1 Cor. 8:13). What is the most common criticism unbelievers level at Christians? Hypocrisy. Christians claim their God is forgiving, yet they refuse to pardon one another. Christians proclaim their God is holy, but their own lives are enmeshed in sin.

Those who do business with you, either as a supervisor, a subordinate, or a client may not always agree with your policies or business strategies, but they should be intrigued by your God. They may clamor for greater profit margins and higher sales performance, but they ought to be satisfied with your integrity. Your honesty and your Christian character should clearly communicate not only that you are a good person but that your God is worthy of your best conduct.

Wise Christian businesspeople recognize that when the day is done, what matters most will not be whether they got their way in the boardroom but whether Christ was glorified through their behavior. At the close of your career, no one will have kept score of how many corporate conflicts you won, but they will remember whether you acted like a genuine Christian. Spiritual statesmen always view their lives and conduct from the vantage point of eternity. Doing so illuminates what is truly important and what is of little consequence.

Because the Spirit of truth lives in you, you should speak the truth in all your business dealings. God graciously forgave your many sins, so how could you hold a grudge against colleagues who disagree with you or challenge you in a meeting? Your God opposes the proud; therefore you ought to be humble in good times and in bad. Regardless of the history your company accumulates under your tenure, people should be able to testify that they know what a godly man or woman looks like as a result of their having worked with you. If they can say this, then they have seen God through your life.

Questions for Reflection

1. How do you represent Christ in your attitudes and your actions at work?
2. How do sins such as anger or greed or pride hinder you from glorifying God in your career?
3. What do you suppose people are learning about God by working with you?
4. What steps might you take so Christ's character becomes more evident through your life?

Additional Resources

Exodus 19:6
Daniel 6:3
Matthew 5:13–16; 7:13–14
1 Peter 2:9–10

Oswald Chambers, *Workmen of God* (London: Oswald Chambers
   Publications: 1937; reprint ed., 1975).
T. W. Hunt, *The Mind of Christ: The Transforming Power of Thinking
   His Thoughts* (Nashville: Broadman and Holman, 1995).
Andrew Murray, *Like Christ* (Springdale, PA: Whitaker House, 1981).
Major Ian Thomas, *The Saving Life of Christ* (Grand Rapids, MI:
   Zondervan Publishing House, 1961; reprint ed., 1982).

How can I stay strong when I'm the only Christian at my workplace?

Scripture warns: "One who isolates himself pursues selfish desires; he rebels against all sound judgment" (Prov. 18:1). Those most vulnerable to moral and ethical downfalls are isolated people. The Scripture encourages: "Two are better than one because they have a good reward for their efforts. For if either falls, his companion can lift him up; but pity the one who falls without another to lift him up. Also, if two lie down together, they can keep warm; but how can one person alone keep warm? And if somebody overpowers one person, two can resist him. A cord of three strands is not easily broken" (Eccles. 4:9–12).

There is tremendous strength in unity between two or more Christians. The encouragement of one friend or colleague can make the difference between success and failure. We all know of high profile CEOs who suffered dramatic scandals and highly publicized downfalls. Friends and colleagues often testify that the disgraced person had previously been viewed as a person of high morals, but his or her integrity was steadily eroded. Sadly, the world watched the tragic debacle of a compromised business leader. Most often, the person gradually pulled back from those who would have offered encouragement and sound advice. This is why believers are exhorted to warn others when we see them drifting into unethical and immoral behavior (Matt. 18:15–20; Gal. 6:1–2). The greater the responsibility you carry, the more critical it is that you make yourself accountable to others.

Your schedule or job assignments may allow for little interaction with other Christians. There may not be any believers in your company or department with whom you can share. You may be surrounded by people who daily press their worldly values and beliefs on you, pushing you to compromise your faith. How then do you submit yourself to someone else who will encourage you to follow through with your convictions?

If you have a heart for living God's way, you will want to ensure that your life is answerable to him (Ps. 25:4–5). Ask God to lead you to a prayer partner. It might be someone you don't know well or perhaps a colleague from a different department. Be alert so God can direct you to that person.

If your spouse is a Christian, you are already blessed with an accountability partner in your home. We both travel a great deal. Both of us call our wives every day. As pressing as our schedules may be, we welcome and need daily contact with our lifetime accountability partner. However, it is also extremely helpful to have a friend or colleague who will walk alongside you. There is no such thing as too much accountability in the Christian life! We never choose to confide in another person *instead* of our wives, but there are unique benefits to having more than one person holding us accountable. Meeting with someone who works in the same field and who faces the same work challenges can be highly encouraging. Obviously, your prayer partner should always be the same gender as you.

If logistics are a problem in meeting with someone, be creative. If you and your prayer partner live or work in different parts of the city, you may choose to meet in the middle, early before traffic gets heavy.

Some people meet once a week, others once a month. Some plan occasional getaways to retreat centers for the purpose of encouraging and challenging each other. For years, Richard and three other men would book rooms for a day at a nearby Christian retreat center. They each spent the morning in their room to meet with God. Then they gathered for lunch to discuss during the afternoon what God had told them. By dinnertime they were on their way home. In this way they were not gone overnight from their families.

Supplementing less frequent meetings by e-mail or phone can also be effective. While nothing can substitute for someone looking you straight in the eye and asking you pointed questions, a certain level of accountability can be achieved long-distance. Technology provides numerous possibilities for two committed friends staying in touch. Webcams allow you to be face-to-face with people on your computer screen though separated by thousands of miles. Text messages from a friend sent to you during challenging moments in your week can help you stay true to your commitments. Anticipating a promised phone call from your prayer partner can uplift you during a particularly trying day.

The key is your desire to be accountable. We can all be tempted to accept our difficulties as insurmountable and give up trying. But a well-timed meeting with a trusted friend can be a powerful catalyst that encourages us to stay the course. Those who cannot find an accountability partner usually do not value the need for one in the first place. Be proactive in making yourself accountable to live with integrity. The reward for such a life is worth any real or imagined scheduling hurdles.

Questions for Reflection

1. Who in your life feels free to ask you difficult accountability questions? If the answer is no one, why is that?
2. Do you tend to avoid accountability, or do you seek it out? What is the evidence?
3. What steps will you take to bring greater accountability into your life? Whom might you ask to be an accountability partner with you?
4. How might technology assist you in keeping yourself accountable to a trusted Christian friend?

Additional Resources

Proverbs 13:20; 14:9; 15:12,22; 17:3,10; 18:1,24; 19:20,25; 21:2; 22:17; 23:9; 23:12; 24:6; 26:12; 27:5,17

Henry Blackaby, *Holiness: God's Plan for Fullness of Life* (Nashville: Thomas Nelson, 2003).

Henry Blackaby and Thomas Blackaby, *Anointed to Be God's Servants: Lessons from the Life of Paul and His Companions* (Nashville: Thomas Nelson, 2005).

Henry Blackaby and Claude King, *Fresh Encounter: Experiencing God Daily through Prayer, Humility and a Heartfelt Desire to Know Him* (Nashville: Broadman and Holman, 1996).

How do I stay humble and still succeed in the fiercely competitive business world?

We like to joke about the fictitious pastor who wrote a book entitled *The Three Greatest Men of God in the Present Era and How I Mentored the Other Two.*

But pride is no laughing matter. It is the most insidious and destructive sin to assault Christian businesspeople. Pride blinds people to danger and predisposes them to calamity. The media showcases the tragic ruination of CEOs and other leaders who blatantly violated their own values and disregarded numerous warning signs about their behavior. These men and women demonstrated remarkable business savvy, but they gradually grew so overconfident in their own abilities or their value to the company that they shunned the warnings of friends and colleagues. In the end, their self-made empire collapsed and their lives crumbled around them.

No person was used by God as mightily in the Old Testament era to influence his generation as Moses. Read his obituary: "No prophet has arisen again in Israel like Moses, whom the LORD knew face to face. He was unparalleled for all the signs and wonders the LORD sent him to do against the land of Egypt—to Pharaoh, to all his officials, and to all his land, and for all the mighty acts of power and terrifying deeds that Moses performed in the sight of all Israel" (Deut. 34:10–12).

What a legacy.

No one was more esteemed in his day than Moses. People knew that by God's awesome power he had parted the Red Sea and reduced the mighty Egyptian Pharaoh and his army to their knees. Moses had faced God on the terrifying Mount Sinai. So Moses could have easily developed an inflated ego, yet this is how Scripture describes him: "Moses was a very humble man, more so than any man on the face of the earth" (Num. 12:3). It is amazing that Moses could participate in such enormous events and yet remain so modest. Of course, his humility is exactly why God used him.

One event in Moses' life particularly shows his unpretentious nature. One day, his faithful servant Joshua discovered two elders, Eldad and Medad, prophesying in the camp. Fearing this would usurp Moses' authority, Joshua urged Moses to command them to stop. Rather than guarding his own prerogative, however, Moses replied: "If only all the LORD's people were prophets, and the LORD would place His Spirit on them" (Num. 11:29). Instead of insisting on his preeminence among the people, Moses wished to honor God by having others do what he had done. That is humility.

In his influential study *Good to Great,* Jim Collins noted that the most successful, "Level Five" leaders are characterized by humility. Humility is not a trait exclusive to Christian businesspeople. It also distinguishes secular leaders who choose to place the well-being of their organizations above their own stature and prosperity. Believers, therefore—because they know God—should without exception be humble men and women.

Humility is not a weakness. Rather, it typifies confident strength, the kind that enables businesspeople to succeed in a competitive, cutthroat market. Moses could remain humble because he knew God would vindicate him (Num. 12:3–5). Moses did not have to worry about promoting his own interests. He was busy advancing God's kingdom.

Humility is the inevitable by-product of an intimate relationship with God. As a Christian, you are unique in the business world. You belong to God. You know him personally. And in knowing the Lord, you come to accurately know yourself. Seeing God as he is brings automatic humility (Isa. 6:5; Rev. 1:17). The more you know him, the more modest you become.

The world tells us: "You can do anything you set your mind to do!" Jesus says, "You can do nothing without me" (John 15:5). Most people in your workplace don't know what you know. That's because Jesus said, "The secrets of the kingdom of heaven have been given for you to know, but it has not been given to them" (Matt. 13:11). Humility reminds you that whatever you have become and whatever you accomplish has been granted to you by God.

People who understand who they are, who know God and his power, can be people of great influence. They are not in bondage to other people's praise and affirmation. Their self-worth comes from their relationship with God. They are not enslaved to temptations that appeal to their pride. They don't put selfish interests above the well-being of their company, employees, and colleagues. They are modest enough to admit when they're wrong and are willing to accept advice. Humble leaders can go about their business with integrity because their definition of success differs from the world's measure. The approval they seek comes from the Lord. The result is that their organization gets their best and God receives the glory.

Additional Resources

Proverbs 3:7, 3:34; 9:8–9; 11:2; 15:33; 16:5, 16:18; 18:12; 25:27; 27:2; 29:23

Isaiah 57:15; 66:2

Matthew 5:5; 20:27–28

Tim Irwin, *Run with the Bulls without Getting Trampled: The Qualities You Need to Stay Out of Harm's Way and Thrive at Work* (Nashville: Thomas Nelson, 2006).

Andrew Murray, *Humility* (New Kensington, PA: Whitaker House, 1982).

How can I find time for spiritual growth and study when I'm this busy?

The moment you stop learning, you cease to grow. The greatest service that leaders can offer the people they lead is to learn. Business challenges, methods, and technology continue to develop at a staggering pace. Anyone who took a new job three years ago and has not kept abreast of the trends in their industry is seriously out-of-date.

As critical as professional development is, spiritual growth is far more important. Yet a hectic career can overshadow our need for Christian growth and crowd out the time required for it.

We are privileged to work with Christian CEOs of Fortune 500 companies. Many of them tell us that although they have extensive educations and often attend world-class seminars, they have never received comprehensive Christian discipleship. They admit they spend inadequate time studying God's Word or reading Christian literature. These top executives are keenly aware of shifting demographic and technological trends as well as geopolitical developments, but they are ignorant of the expectations Almighty God has for them. They are oblivious to what God is currently doing in the world around them. But they *want* to know God's heart. The question is, where do they start?

The following are some guidelines you might find helpful as you strive to enhance your Bible knowledge and enrich your spiritual life:

1. Be intentional about your spiritual growth. Develop a plan. Set aside specific times to read and engage in serious study. Set goals for yourself. ("I will read one helpful book each week.")

2. Free up space in your life so you have time to read. We are bewildered by pastors and businesspeople who bemoan their lack of time for reading Christian literature, but they can analyze the Monday night football game in minute detail or enthusiastically discuss the latest movies and TV shows. Spiritual growth occurs when it is a priority. Otherwise, almost anything will take its place in our busy lives. Clearly, there is not enough time to do *everything* you would like to do each week, so you must make hard choices with your schedule. Every time you reach for the TV remote, pick up a Christian classic book instead and see how it enriches your life.

3. Use technology to help you. Numerous innovative ways to learn are at your fingertips. Listen to audiobooks as you commute to work. Study Scripture resources on your laptop when you are on a plane *en route* to a meeting. Handhelds can store Scripture and various devotional books you can read while waiting to meet someone. Innumerable innovative resources are available to you if you are serious about spiritual growth.

4. Join a learning cluster. Find people who want to grow in their Bible knowledge, too, and organize yourselves to study together. We work with groups of ten to fifteen CEOs at a time that meet with us three times a year in a particular city, such as St. Louis, Dallas, Denver, or Atlanta. We convene at a hotel near the airport for a concentrated period of teaching that occurs over a twenty-four-hour period. These busy CEOs schedule time to fly to the designated city and to undergo intensive training on being spiritual statesmen in the marketplace. Then they return home to carry on their business responsibilities. This is a significant sacrifice, but you should hear their stories as God completely reshapes them, their priorities, and the way they conduct their lives. If you spend time with other business leaders who are taking their learning seriously, you will be inspired to do the same.

5. *Surround yourself with learners* who also want to grow in their personal, professional, and spiritual lives. Seek out the avid readers in your church and ask them to recommend books that will help you grow in your faith. Approach the thinkers within your Christian community and have in-depth discussions with them. Far too many people are satisfied with the status quo. Don't let these unmotivated people deaden your desire to grow spiritually.

It is indeed a challenge to keep learning while also holding a busy, highly demanding job. But there are ways, so persevere. God wants you to mature in your understanding of him and his Word. He will guide you so you continue to learn despite your responsibilities and pressures.

Questions for Reflection

1. What particular knowledge or skill are you presently seeking? If there is nothing specific, ask God what he wants you to learn this year.
2. Do you follow a plan to ensure you are daily learning and growing? If not, what could such a plan look like?
3. What time and budget have you set aside for spiritual learning this year? Is there a conference you could attend? A place of retreat for study and meditation?
4. What kind of people do you gravitate toward—those who are constantly growing, or those who have stagnated? Who are some keen thinkers and learners with whom you could spend more time?

5. What was the last book you read that deeply challenged you and the way you act? What book could you begin reading this week that might significantly enrich your life?

Additional Resources

Proverbs 19:20–21; 24:6
Ephesians 3:14–21; 5:15–17, 21

Richard Blackaby, *Unlimiting God: Increasing Your Capacity to Experience the Divine* (Colorado Springs: Multnomah, 2008).
Gordon MacDonald, *Ordering Your Private World* (Nashville: Thomas Nelson, 1984).
Richard A. Swenson, *Margin: Restoring Emotional, Physical, Financial, and Time Reserves to Overloaded Lives* (Colorado Springs: NavPress, 1992).

How do I maintain a devotional life when I'm constantly traveling?

Travel is the bane of many a businessperson's existence. It impedes healthy routines. Traveling through different time zones is wearying. Navigating airport check-in, security, and customs; renting cars; finding hotels; and eating in restaurants can consume many hours. Traveling business leaders with such a grueling itinerary must work hard to maintain their devotional life.

While it is certainly easier to spend regular time with God when you follow a predictable weekly routine, understanding several truths can help you maintain your devotional life regardless of the unique demands of business travel.

Remember that God does not "join you" when you have a quiet time. He is always present. His Holy Spirit lives within you. Your devotional time should be a special, focused, uninterrupted encounter with God, but that is not the only part of your day when God is present. Be alert to recognize all that God is doing around you as you walk with him throughout the day.

You might chat with a nonbeliever sitting next to you on the airplane and afterward praise God that he gave you his words to share. Pay attention to the many ways God watches over the details of your travel. When you are stuck in an endless line to clear airport security or customs, you may hear disgruntled passengers berating airport employees for the inconvenience. Silently thank God that he helps you recognize what is important and what is not, and take this opportunity to offer a pleasant word of encouragement. Ask God by his grace to keep you free from anger and instead to make you his ambassador in the high-stress world of business travel.

Use your down time to communicate with God. Flights can be anything but tranquil, but they may provide welcome times of stillness before the Lord. Spend those moments praying and reflecting on what God is doing in your life. (Certainly, turbulence can help usher you into a prayerful frame of mind!) Businesspeople often seize the opportunity to work on business during a flight, but you could also use travel time to read your Bible or listen to Christian CDs. Keep an uplifting book in your carry-on luggage. We've discovered that boarding passes make great bookmarks!

Hotel rooms can be lonely places, but you can use the solitude to have special times with God. Business traveling often brings a full schedule including breakfast, lunch, and dinner meetings. But you may find discretionary time to employ for a personal spiritual retreat. Businesspeople often travel to various venues having already investigated the local golf courses or sports teams. Or they will spend spare time at the tennis courts, in the swimming pool, or in the exercise room. These are all great ways to relax or to keep fit while on the road. But a hotel setting can also provide a place of privacy for a profound encounter with God. That insidious time gobbler in your hotel room, the television, can be left off. You don't have to fill the airspace with noise or pollute your brain with mind-numbing shows. We make a habit never to turn on the TV in our hotel rooms. If it's not on, there is no temptation to channel surf or stay up too late. At home you might be bombarded with the busyness of your regular schedule, but being alone out of town can allow for uninterrupted time with God. Try scheduling a quiet time with God at your next hotel stay.

If you plan wisely, business travel can enrich your Christian life. There are many wonderful churches in cities where you may be doing business. For example, if you are in New York City, you might visit the prayer meeting at Brooklyn Tabernacle. Don't just find out what professional sports team is in town; also consider worshipping at a local church. Perhaps visiting the service of a different denomination than your own will open your heart to new worship experiences. If you are traveling in Europe, you might seek out historic sites where devout Christians were martyred for their faith. In the Middle East, many biblical sites could help make Scripture come alive to you. When traveling, make an effort to contact believers in that part of the world. Such encounters can change your life. Many devout Christians around the world could inspire you with their stories. You could also render a blessing by seeking to encourage local believers wherever you are.

Conclusion

Don't allow travel to serve as an excuse for neglecting your devotional life. Business trips cannot prevent you from spending time with God. They merely reveal how important time with God is to you. Travel can greatly enhance your walk with God if you are intentional in your planning.

Questions for Reflection

1. Does travel adversely affect your spiritual life? If so, how?
2. As you reflect on the kind of travel you do, how might you capitalize on your schedule to enrich your devotional life?

3. What are some tools, such as Bible software programs, that you might obtain to make God's Word more accessible when you're on the road?
4. Are there some travel behaviors or habits you should cease in order to enhance your devotional life?

Additional Resources

Jeremiah 6:10; 7:13; 29:11–14; 33:3
Mark 1:35
Luke 21:36
Ephesians 5:15–17

Arthur Bennett, ed., *The Valley of Vision: A Collection of Puritan Prayers and Devotions* (Carlisle, PA: The Banner of Truth Trust, 1975; reprint ed., 1995).

Henry Blackaby and Richard Blackaby, *Discovering God's Daily Agenda* (Nashville: Thomas Nelson, 2007).

Henry Blackaby and Richard Blackaby, *Experiencing God: Day by Day* (Nashville: Broadman and Holman, 1997).

Oswald Chambers, *My Utmost for His Highest* (New York: Dodd, Mead and Company, 1935; 58th printing).

Dan Crawford, *The Prayer Shaped Disciple* (Peabody, MA: Hendricksen Publishers, 1999).

Ron Eggert, *Tozer on Christian Leadership: A 366-Day Devotional* (Camp Hill, PA: Christian Publications, Inc., 2001).

Donald Whitney, *Spiritual Disciplines for the Christian Life* (Colorado Springs: NavPress, 1996).

I haven't been a very good Christian example at work. How do I start now?

We often meet Christian businesspeople who feel convicted about the way they've behaved at work. Some, who were not believers when they first joined their company, developed questionable work habits and reputations that are now difficult to discard. Others were Christians, but they did not previously understand how their divine calling impacted their job performance. They valued climbing the corporate ladder, even at the expense of others, rather than bringing glory to God. Now the Holy Spirit is convicting them of their behavior, and they want to know what to do. Here are some suggestions:

Be quick to repent of your actions. Repentance is a life change. It involves a 180 degree shift in direction. To repent means to agree with God about your sin and to make the adjustments God commands. Having the ability to repent means we are not slaves to our destructive behavior. We are always one sincere, repentant prayer away from being set free from our harmful habits. If you want God to change your image at work, begin by sincerely repenting of your past behavior. If you empty yourself of ungodly habits, you will be prepared to fill your life with healthy, God-honoring routines.

Ask God to help you be reconciled with anyone at work whom you may have harmed. Your words or behavior may have injured your coworkers, and your negative example may have been a deterrent to non-Christians in your company. Having seen your conduct as a Christian, they may have concluded that Christianity is not for them. Scripture has harsh words for people who are stumbling blocks to others (Matt. 18:6; 23:13; 1 Cor. 8:9). It may be that your unchristlike behavior at work has caused people to turn away from Christ and the salvation he offers. Take this matter seriously and seek to rectify it immediately.

A highly challenging Scripture is found in the book of Ezekiel. The Israelites were supposed to be holy witnesses to all the nations of the earth, reflecting God's greatness. Instead they succumbed to greed and immorality. The result was that God's people actually harmed his reputation rather than glorified his name. This is what God declared:

> Then I had concern for My holy name, which the house
> of Israel profaned among the nations where they went.
> Therefore, say to the house of Israel: This is what the
> Lord GOD says: It is not for your sake that I will act, house
> of Israel, but for My holy name, which you profaned among
> the nations where you went. I will honor the holiness of My
> great name, which has been profaned among the nations—the
> name you have profaned among them. The nations will know
> that I am Yahweh—the declaration of the Lord GOD—when
> I demonstrate My holiness through you in their sight.
> For I will take you from the nations and gather you from
> all the countries, and will bring you into your own land. I will
> also sprinkle clean water on you, and you will be clean. I will
> cleanse you from all your impurities and all your idols. I will
> give you a new heart and put a new spirit within you; I will
> remove your heart of stone and give you a heart of flesh. I will

place My spirit within you and cause you to follow My statutes and carefully observe My ordinances. Then you will live in the land that I gave your fathers; you will be My people, and I will be your God. I will save you from all your uncleanness. I will summon the grain and make it plentiful, and will not bring famine on you. I will also make the fruit of the trees and the produce of the field plentiful, so that you will no longer experience reproach among the nations on account of famine.

Then you will remember your evil ways and your deeds that were not good, and you will loathe yourselves for your iniquities and abominations. It is not for your sake that I will act—the declaration of the Lord GOD—let this be known to you. Be ashamed and humiliated because of your ways, house of Israel!

This is what the Lord GOD says: On the day I cleanse you from all your iniquities, I will cause the cities to be inhabited, and the ruins will be rebuilt. The desolate land will be cultivated instead of lying desolate in the sight of everyone who passes by. Then they will say: This land that was desolate has become like the garden of Eden. The cities that were once ruined, desolate, and destroyed are now fortified and inhabited. Then the nations that remain around you will know that I, the LORD, have rebuilt what was destroyed and have replanted what was desolate. I, the LORD, have spoken and I will do it. (Ezek. 36:21–36)

God is concerned for his reputation. He will not tolerate his people misrepresenting him. If we choose to live unholy lives and flagrantly ignore God's ways, then he will deal with our sin severely. When God's people return to him, however, he will give us new hearts and restore our fellowship with him.

If you have been carelessly misrepresenting God to others, be assured that God takes your behavior seriously. If you have offended people at work, apologize to them and do whatever is necessary to be reconciled with them (Luke 19:8). Such an action on your part might alert them that they have not been seeing true Christianity in you to this point. It may also help hold you accountable not to slip back into your previous sinful habits.

Godliness is not something you only practice at church. Righteousness is lived out in the context of your daily activity. Ask God to develop godliness in your life. Only he can do this (Gal. 5:16). It is one thing to express regret for your past behavior. It is another to begin living a radically different life before your coworkers. Only the Holy Spirit can make you think and act like Jesus. He will not force godliness upon you. But if you ask God to make you blameless in your relationships and in your actions at work, he will clearly guide you into righteous living.

Once you surrender your life into Gods hands, *expect* things to change. If you were previously known for your fiery temper, watch for God to help you deal with frustrations in a Christlike way. If you habitually hurled caustic comments at underperforming employees, recognize new opportunities to show godly patience. Godliness is like a muscle; it needs exercise. If you want to be more gracious, don't expect God to remove every irritating situation from your life. Rather, God may present plenty of opportunities for you to represent his character to a watching world.

Never lose hope just because you have not behaved righteously at work in the past. The apostle Paul was spiritually blind in his early adult years. He vehemently attacked Christianity in his misguided sense of what pleased God. But when he realized what he had done, he chose to relinquish his chosen career and to pursue God's will for his life (Phil. 3:13). Likewise, you cannot undo your past, but you can choose to behave in a godly manner today. Don't just *decide* to live differently. Repent of your unchristlike example and begin to *act* righteously now as God enables you.

Questions for Reflection

1. Has your past conduct at work been dishonoring to God? If so, how?
2. What specific steps is God leading you to make to rectify your past behavior? Are there people with whom you need to be reconciled?
3. What areas of your life does God want to make more Christlike?

Additional Resources

Henry Blackaby and Claude King, *Fresh Encounter: Experiencing God through Prayer, Humility, and a Heartfelt Desire to Know Him* (Nashville: Broadman and Holman, 1996).

Henry Blackaby, *Holiness: God's Plan for Fulness of Life* (Nashville: Thomas Nelson, 2003).

Nancy Leigh DeMoss, *Holiness: The Heart God Purifies* (Chicago: Moody Publishers, 2004).

John Hunter, *Limiting God* (Grand Rapids, MI: Zondervan, 1966; reprint ed., Kingsport, TN: Fresh Springs Publications, 1995).

Chip Ingram, *Holy Transformation: What It Takes for God to Make a Difference in You* (Chicago: Moody Publishers, 2003).

Charles G. Trumbull, *Victory in Christ* (Fort Washington, PA: Christian Literature Crusade, 1959).

How do I know if God is calling me out of the business world and into Christian ministry?

The call of God is primarily to a relationship with him. Where God assigns you, of course, is up to him and is sacred. Wherever God has called you, you are his missionary and are already in full-time ministry. Churches ought to commission and pray for schoolteachers, doctors, nurses, and businesspeople as they enter the mission fields where they work, just as they do for those who travel overseas in God's service.

Nonetheless, God does call some people to leave their place of employ and to enter the ministry as a shepherd to his people. The Bible holds numerous examples of God doing this. Most notably, Jesus called his disciples, who were businessmen, to leave their trades and to follow him (Luke 5:10–11). Peter, Andrew, James, and John were career fishermen. Theirs was a relatively stable, secure profession. Jesus called them to spend their days fishing for eternal souls instead (Mark 1:16–20). Matthew was a tax official, but he abandoned that job to become an apostle (Luke 5:27–28). These men could not continue earning their living the way they had and accomplish all God intended through them for his kingdom.

The question is, how would you know if God is leading you away from your current profession and into some form of full-time ministry? There are several crucial considerations:

Carefully examine what God has been doing in your life. Has he sensitized your heart and drawn your attention to specific ministry concerns? How has he been using your life for his kingdom purposes? For example, has God led you into leadership positions in your church? Has he used you to bring others to faith in Christ? Has he encouraged people in their faith through you? Do people seek you out for spiritual counsel and guidance? Has God been working through you to build up his church? How does your church staff view your contribution to your church? Are you an encouragement to them? Have you been asked to preach, teach, or share your testimony? If so, what happened when you did? Have fellow believers affirmed God's hand on your life? Have the results of your obedience to God been positive? Have you experienced an exhilarating sense of joy when you have ministered in Christ's name?

If God is setting you apart for a particular service, others will also recognize God's activity in your life. In fact, other church members may often identify God's activity in your life before you do. That is because they recognize how God encourages them when you preach or teach the Bible, pray for them, or visit them. Likewise, a spiritually astute ministerial staff will notice when God is using one of their members extensively to edify the church. If you feel God may be calling you, you should talk with your pastor and relate what you're sensing.

At times a godly layperson is reassigned by God. We know many successful businesspeople who felt called into ministerial assignments. Many of the finest students who come to our seminaries are leaving prosperous careers to obey God's call. They had been faithful in all God put before them previously, and now God is giving them a fresh, challenging assignment in his kingdom. After Peter and his partners experienced their greatest single catch of fish, Jesus called them to walk away from their business (Luke 5:10). Christian ministry is not for those who merely want to escape their current professions. God wants his choice servants to represent him and minister to his people. God may allow you to experience significant business success before he reassigns you. Do not erroneously assume that business profits are a sign that you should stay where you are. You must settle the fact that your motivation in life is not closing the biggest deal or making the most money but obeying the Lord.

At times people experience a holy restlessness that they can't explain, but they sense God is releasing them from their current work to do something new. This is not because they are failing where they are. It is a God-initiated stirring in their heart. Numerous ministers began their careers as businesspeople, but God reassigned them to serve on staff in churches. Not surprisingly, people from the corporate world are finding Christ through the ministries of these former business leaders. Because of their previous experience, these ministers know how to lead their churches to reach out to men and women in the business sector.

Unfortunately, our religious culture has created unbiblical terminology. "Full-time ministry" (meaning a pastor, church staff person, or international missionary) has cultural implications. When God calls someone, God also prepares that person. But at times North American culture acts as if only those who have a theological degree and who are paid full-time by a church or mission agency are ministers. In reality, every believer is a priest (1 Pet. 2:9) and Christ's ambassador (2 Cor. 5:20). God's assignments for you will not be determined by whether you've graduated from a divinity school or can translate Scripture from the original Hebrew but by your intimate, obedient walk with him. Each of us must ask God to show us how he wants to use our lives to minister to others.

Questions for Reflection

1. What is your sense of divine call to the job you now hold? Are you currently experiencing a sense of spiritual restlessness? Is God releasing you from your present assignment and responsibilities?
2. How is God using your life to build up his church? How do people respond when you minister to them?
3. Have fellow believers sensed that you may be called into ministry? Has a pastor suggested this to you?
4. If you sense God may be reassigning you out of the business world and into a ministry role, what do you plan to do next?

Additional Resources

Genesis 12:1–4
Exodus 3:1–11; 35:30–36:2
John 1:35–51
Acts 9:1–19

Henry Blackaby, *Created to Be God's Friend: How God Shapes Those He Loves* (Nashville: Thomas Nelson, 1999).

Henry Blackaby, *Chosen to Be God's Prophet: Lessons from the Life of Samuel* (Nashville: Thomas Nelson, 2003).

Henry Blackaby and Henry Brandt, *The Power of the Call* (Nashville: Broadman and Holman, 1997).

Henry Blackaby and Norman Blackaby, *Called and Accountable: Discovering Your Place in God's Eternal Purpose,* revised ed. (Birmingham, AL: New Hope Publishers, 2005).

Oswald Chambers, *Called of God* (Fort Washington, PA: Christian Literature Crusade, 1965; reprint ed., 1975).

Wesley L. Duewel, *Ablaze for God* (Grand Rapids, MI: Francis Asbury Press, 1989).

Ron F. Wagley
Chairman, CEO, and President (Retired)
Transamerica Occidental Life
Insurance Company

Is God in the marketplace? Does God even care? Or is he at odds with the marketplace? And what about those in the marketplace who are committed to serving him while at the same time are charged with pleasing their employers? Is that even possible?

It would be wrong to think that you cannot be a Christian in today's business world. When you consider the unethical and criminal behavior of some corporate leaders over the last few years, businesses need Christians who apply biblical principles and have a growing relationship with Jesus Christ that translates itself into their life, one that affects how they perform their jobs with integrity and a strong sense of ethics and values, regardless of position.

I wish that I could tell you I've always had this mind-set, but that wouldn't be true. When I got out of college, my "Christianity" could best be described as "stained glass." In other words, although I had become a Christian as a youth, I regarded Christianity as a "church thing" that belonged behind stained glass windows. Faith had no place or relevance to the outside world, particularly for one anxious to climb the world's ladder of success. My focus was on pursuing the "American Dream," which translated into getting more things. Isn't that the world's message and definition of success?

"Getting" determined my values and priorities, and therefore, any contentment or sense of fulfillment was typically short-lived and circumstantial. "Getting" was never enough to satisfy, however, and it never came quickly enough! My life was characterized by varying degrees of frustration. The thought of settling for something less than the "American Dream" frustrated me even more and caused me to redouble my efforts to achieve. This only caused more frustration.

During this time, I never gave much thought to my Christian faith except for occasional panic or self-centered prayers for God to get me what I wanted. I treated God as if he were a magical, on-call genie-in-a-bottle that, when all else failed, I could pray and appeal to. But even then, he seemed distant and impersonal. It was all about me.

All this changed when my wife and I joined a home Bible study. God began to deal with me through his Word. I had never personally studied the Bible but respected it as a good religious book. There were times when I felt drawn to it but found it hard to understand. Its relevance escaped me because I had never met anyone who seriously applied the Bible to their life and career.

Over time and with the help of a patient study leader, my thinking was revolutionized. For the first time I was shown how to study God's Word, not as some intellectual endeavor but rather to determine what specific Scriptures said, what they meant, and (most importantly) what they meant to me in terms of personal application. I slowly began to integrate my faith and biblical principles into my marriage, my family, and my career and corporate positions.

The latter didn't come easy.

I once heard, "If your faith doesn't make a difference in the things that make a difference, then what's the difference?"

For me, the area that made the biggest difference in my life, aside from my marriage and family, was my corporate business career. And it was overdue for God's overhauling!

The Bible tells me to do my work as unto the Lord, not man (Eph. 6:7). This did away with office politics and shifted my career perspective on getting ahead. No longer could I be upset, complain, and be critical for not getting a raise or promotion when God was my real boss! I began to shift my focus to the quality of my work, because I wanted to do my very best not just to please men but now to please God and leave the results to him.

With this shift I came to realize that my witness for Christ was made more effective by the quality of my work and by striving to be a great employee. Slip-shod performance diminishes one's testimony, whereas setting and achieving high quality standards becomes a platform to witness and give God glory.

I do recall, however, that when I began to develop a hunger for studying God's Word, I found that my professional studies interfered with this desire. I remember complaining about this to a fellow believer, a well-respected and successful architect, expecting him to agree and counsel me to back off of my business studies and focus on the spiritual. Surprisingly, he chided me and told me that he believed his first step in witnessing was to become the very best architect in the city, and that this fact would earn him a platform for being a strong witness.

That really resonated with me.

I discovered that God doesn't view my life as being compartmentalized. His purpose in giving us his Word is to equip us for "every good work" (2 Tim. 3:16–17), This applies to behavior and good work for him on the job as well as in outside activities. The basis of my integrity should be the consistent application of his words, principles, and commands in every part of my life.

Over time, as God's Word began to change my values and priorities, I realized that I couldn't be or act the way God desired in my own strength. I reached the point where I had to admit to him that if this was what he wanted, then he would have to provide the strength and courage, because it was beyond me! I wanted to change and be content with an attitude of thanksgiving. So I committed to him my career, job, salary, position, performance, and business future—all of it—and told him I would accept the results, no matter what, and just try each day to be a good ambassador for him.

I began to make an attempt to be sensitive to people regardless of their position and try to help whenever possible, particularly in crisis situations. After all, there is no distinction in God's eyes between senior corporate officers or janitors. Résumés, education, or titles don't mean much to God, who places great value on everyone. I discovered that you don't need to go out of your way to find people who need help and need to hear about God and Jesus Christ. If and when someone would ask "why," then I felt I had the liberty to share my faith. The world doesn't have answers for those in crisis situations, but God does. Looking at my daily life and career in this way was revolutionary for me.

Only by God's grace have I been allowed to occupy positions of leadership in the corporate world. I am amazed at what God has done. He certainly did a much better job with me than I ever did! It seemed that when I changed my focus, that's when he began his work in me. I give God all the glory.

Seven years ago, I was made head of one of the world's largest financial services corporations. With blessings come responsibilities, and my perspective is now one of stewardship to use what he has allowed as a platform for accomplishing his unchanging mission of glorifying himself and expanding his kingdom.

It's no longer about me; it really is about him. My story is one of changing my focus from one of "getting" to one of "giving" God his proper place in my life, as well as in the marketplace!

RON WAGLEY recently retired as chairman, CEO, and president of Transamerica Occidental Life Insurance Company. He and his wife, Saundra, live in Westlake Village, California, where they are active in church ministries, leading discipleship groups, and directing a foundation for helping abused women and children. Ron speaks regularly to university students on leadership and lessons learned from his forty years of corporate life. They enjoy their two married children and four wonderful grandchildren.

PART 2

My Business Life

When Moses stood before the burning bush, he was in the midst of his workday, herding sheep. God called to him and said, "Take your sandals off your feet, for the place where you are standing is holy ground" (Exod. 3:5). What made this ordinary workplace holy ground? God's presence. Wherever God is, that place is sacred.

Jesus said, "The one who welcomes you welcomes Me, and the one who welcomes Me welcomes Him who sent Me" (Matt. 10:40). Paul reminded believers that their body was the Holy Spirit's temple (1 Cor. 6:19–20). If you are a Christian, God dwells within you. Whether you are in a boardroom, on an airplane, or in a client's office, God is there too. There are no secular places in your life because holy God abides within you.

How do I apply biblical principles to my business?

The Bible offers plenty of instruction regarding business success:

1. Whatever you do in word or in deed, do it for the Lord (Prov. 3:5; 1 Cor. 10:31; 2 Cor. 5:9; Eph. 5:15–17; Col. 3:17). As you perform your job, realize you are living for Christ. He should receive honor through your career just as he does through your church involvement. As a Christian, you are a spiritual being; therefore your work life is as spiritual as your devotional life. It all belongs to God.

2. Do all things without complaining and disputing (Phil. 2:14). Don't be a whiner. The world has plenty of critics and complainers. Keep a positive spirit. You know the Lord. No problem is beyond his power.

3. Be humble (Prov. 11:2; 16:5; 29:23; Phil. 2:5–8). Follow Jesus' example: Christ relinquished his heavenly throne to live as a commoner among the people he had created. Even secular leadership pundits recognize that great leaders are humble people who make the places they lead great.

4. Watch what you say (Prov. 8:8; 10:19–21; 15:23,26; 16:13; 25:15; Eph. 4:29; Col. 4:6; James 3:1–12). Words aptly chosen can encourage and energize others. Careless talk can debilitate you or your listener. Don't speak rashly. Think before you speak. Be mindful how you address others. Do you tend to inspire people, or injure them? Winning an argument gives fleeting gratification, but winning a friend brings lasting satisfaction.

5. *Keep learning* (Prov. 1:5). Smart leaders realize there is much they don't know. Keep reading, studying, and seeking advice. Maintain a teachable spirit. Don't let pride hinder you from growing spiritually. The Bible is a treasure trove of wisdom, and even secular leaders are discovering that biblical principles make solid business sense. As a businessperson, you can't afford *not* to know God's Word.

6. *Guard your integrity* (Ps. 18:23; 26:11; 37:37; 41:12; Prov. 2:7; 11:8). Whether you're in politics, the professional sector, the marketplace, or church ministry, you are an ambassador for Christ. The competitive drive in leaders can tempt them to compromise their principles if the outcome looks appealing. Don't do it. Your integrity is priceless. Don't allow anyone or anything to dismantle it. God's Word is filled with promises for those who honor him (1 Sam. 2:30). Scripture warns us that if we pervert our way, we *will* eventually be found out (Prov. 10:9; Eccles. 10:1).

7. *Work hard!* (Prov. 10:4; 21:5; 27:23). Don't spend your days scheming shortcuts to success. The reason many people underachieve is that they are not willing to pay the price of hard work. Lazy people do not impact the world for good. Rather, they have a negative effect on those in their sphere of influence. Ask God for his evaluation of your work ethic.

8. *Seek good counsel* (Prov. 11:14; 13:18). Good advice is invaluable. The wisdom of a godly colleague can save you from disaster. You must be teachable, however, to benefit from counselors. Be proactive. Enlist a group of wise friends to help you process ideas and issues. Don't be like King Rehoboam who ignored sage instruction and listened instead to people who led him to his ruin (1 Kings 12:1–20). Only fools isolate themselves from those who will tell them the truth (Prov. 18:1).

9. *Honor the Lord with your wealth* (Prov. 3:9; 11:25). Can God trust you with riches? Some Christian businesspeople seek wealth simply to improve their lifestyle. Others have a greater vision for their earnings— investing in God's kingdom. Your decisions in this regard will set you apart from secular magnates. While many non-Christian businesspeople are

philanthropic according to their personal interests, Christians give generously as God directs, knowing he will lead them to invest in eternity. Jesus urged: "Give, and it will be given to you; a good measure—pressed down, shaken together, and running over—will be poured into your lap. For with the measure you use, it will be measured back to you" (Luke 6:38).

10. Show mercy (Prov. 11:17). Running a business or leading an organization requires some tough calls, but as you seek to improve your company's standing, never forget to show mercy. You are where you are by God's grace. It *is* possible to succeed in competitive markets while being gracious (Mic. 6:8).

11. Control your anger (Prov. 15:18; 16:32; 29:11; Col. 3:8). Many leaders have lost everything because they could not control their temper. Anger is a deadly sin. Fury blinds people to what is important. Resentment eats away at your soul. Wrath destroys relationships, causing otherwise intelligent people to say foolish, devastating things. Anger has no place in a Christian leader's life.

12. Don't fear people (Prov. 29:25). God is the only One a spiritual leader should fear. He is the One who will eventually hold everyone accountable for their actions (2 Cor. 5:10). Letting people intimidate you makes you vulnerable to compromising your faith and integrity. God has not given you a spirit of fear, but of power and love and a sound mind (2 Tim. 1:7). Don't live in fear. Follow your Christian convictions and allow God to vindicate you in his own way.

Questions for Reflection

1. Are any of the preceding principles lacking in your life?
2. Which of these twelve truths could God work into your life right now?
3. What actions will you take to make these principles a part of your life?

Additional Resources

Proverbs 1:5; 3:5–6; 4:20–27; 10
Matthew 7:24–29; 10:32–33; 16:24–27; 25:14–30
Mark 1:16–20; 4:21–25; 8:34–38; 10:17–31; 12:41–44
Luke 18:18–30
1 Corinthians 15:10
James 1:5,19; 4:17
1 Peter 2:9–10

Randy Alcorn, *The Treasure Principle: Discovering the Secret of Joyful Giving* (Sisters, OR: Multnomah, 2001).

John D. Beckett, *Loving Monday: Succeeding in Business Without Selling Your Soul* (Downers Grove, IL: InterVarsity Press, 1998).

John D. Beckett, *Mastering Monday: A Guide to Integrating Faith and Work* (Downers Grove, IL: InterVarsity Press, 2006).

Ken Blanchard and S. Truett Cathy, *The Generosity Factor: Discover the Joy of Giving Your Time, Talent, and Treasure* (Grand Rapids, MI: Zondervan, 2002).

Ron Blue, *Generous Living: Finding Contentment through Giving* (Grand Rapids, MI: Zondervan, 1997).

Joe Calhoon and Bruce Jeffrey, *Prioritize! A System for Leading Your Business and Life on Purpose* (Sevierville, TN: Insight, 2005).

Regi Campbell, *About My Father's Business: Taking Your Faith to Work* (Sisters, OR: Multnomah, 2005).

Alan Gotthardt, *The Eternity Portfolio: A Practical Guide to Investing Your Money for Ultimate Results* (Wheaton: Tyndale House Publishing, 2003).

Kent Humphries, *Lasting Investments: A Pastor's Guide for Equipping Workplace Leaders to Leave a Spiritual Legacy* (Colorado Springs: NavPress, 2004).

Does God really care about my business decisions?

Professional people may think praying for God to guide and bless their business is worldly or downright selfish. Many Christians hesitate to ask fellow believers for prayer as they make significant business decisions because they don't want to appear self-seeking.

That's because we tend to divide life into two categories: the sacred and the secular. Sometimes we assume God is only concerned with sanctified issues such as the church, evangelism, and missions. We surmise he is ambivalent toward such earthly cares as business, politics, and education. God, however, does not operate in a dichotomy as we do. *Everything* is sacred to God! The whole world is the arena of his divine activity.

God designed humanity and all his creation to glorify him. There are no parameters to the ways and means God wants to express his love. No boundaries limit him from bringing about his eternal plan for humanity's redemption. Your business, then, is a channel through which God can receive honor, a voice through which he can express his love for people, and a conduit through which he can deliver grace to those who need salvation.

If you view your company as secular, you may succumb to greed and questionable ethics or exploit your employees, which will discredit your Christian witness. By artificially categorizing your career as separate from your Christian life, you are not only dishonoring God, you are likely subjecting yourself to failure. Why? Because as a Christian, you carry God's holy name with you. If your life dishonors him, God will deal with you so he is honored through you (Ezek. 36:16–38). Numerous Christian executives have testified that it took financial and professional disaster to reorient them from pursuing worldly goals to putting God first.

Fortunately, a growing number of businesspeople are wholly submitting their work life to the Lord. Businesspeople give generously to God's kingdom work, supporting missions and various ministries. Compassionate Christians administer corporate profits to better the lives of their employees. We know several leaders of sizable companies who, accustomed to thinking globally, use their significant resources to invest in the betterment of Third World countries.

The ways to serve and honor God through your business are limitless. In the same light, don't rule out the reality that God may choose to bless your enterprises extensively. When you willingly honor God through your leadership, he may choose to guide you to remarkable success. John Beckett of R. W. Beckett Corporation and Truett Cathey of Chic-Fil-A, both successful business owners, have invested large portions of their profits into God's kingdom work. Both men humbly recount occasions when God specifically guided them in their business decisions, resulting in increased profitability and greater resources for expressing God's love to others.

When God chose to bless Abraham, it was so Abraham could be a blessing to the families of the earth (Gen. 12:1). When God gave Joseph insights into the national economy, it was so he could save tens of thousands of people from starvation during a drought. The result of Joseph's acumen brought honor to God and accomplished his purposes (Gen. 41). The Scriptures cite numerous men and women whose business prowess came from God, was used for his glory, and was directed to his purposes. Abraham mobilized his employees to free people from captivity (Gen. 14:14). Joseph of Arimathea leveraged his wealth to provide a tomb for Jesus (Matt. 27:57–60). Mary, the mother of John Mark, offered her spacious residence to host gatherings of the early church (Acts 12:12). The business-woman Lydia used her home to host the missionaries Paul and Barnabas (Acts 16:11–15). Archippus hosted a church in his home (Philem. 2).

God is *absolutely* concerned with the business choices you make. He expects his people to be a beacon of hope in a decaying, darkened world (Matt. 5:13–16). Those who conduct business are in a unique position to honor God. Don't call your work secular. It is (or can be) a vibrant, integral component of your Christian walk. Welcome God into your office. Seek his wisdom and trust his leading.

Questions for Reflection

1. What role does God have in your business decisions? How significant does a decision have to be for you to classify it as worthy of prayer?
2. How long are you willing to wait for God's guidance before you move forward with a business decision?
3. What areas in your business life are lacking God's guidance? What can you do to change that?

Additional Resources

Genesis 13:14–18; 15:1

2 Chronicles 16:9

Psalms 8:4; 11:1–7; 15:1–2; 16:7–8; 18:36; 20:7; 25:3; 34:4; 37:3–5, 37:23–25, 37:37; 40:4; 48:14; 56:4; 61:8; 73:24; 127:1

Proverbs 3:5–6; 4:23

Henry Blackaby and Richard Blackaby, *Spiritual Leadership: Moving People on to God's Agenda* (Nashville: Broadman and Holman, 2001).

John D. Beckett, *Loving Monday: Succeeding in Business without Selling Your Soul* (Downers Grove, IL: InterVarsity Press, 1998).

John D. Beckett, *Mastering Monday: A Guide to Integrating Faith and Work* (Downers Grove, IL: InterVarsity Press, 2006).

Regi Campbell, *About My Father's Business: Taking Your Faith to Work* (Sisters, OR: Multnomah, 2005).

Truett Cathy, *It's Easier to Succeed than to Fail* (Nashville: Oliver Nelson, 1989).

How should I pray for my business?

Praying for your business is the most crucial aspect of your position as a Christian leader. Scripture admonishes "in everything, through prayer and petition with thanksgiving, let your requests be made known to God" (Phil. 4:6). No part of your life should be excluded from prayer.

Probably no area of your life is as pressured by the world as your business. Carnal morals and attitudes daily bombard the workplace. Christian values are constantly questioned and mocked. If you do not cover it with prayer, your job can become the fissure through which deadly sins seep into your life. The apostle Paul urged believers not to be "conformed to this age" but to be transformed by the renewing of their minds (Rom. 12:2). Too many believers have allowed their values and attitudes to be shaped by the same mold as their nonbelieving colleagues until they become indistinguishable from them. Through prayer you can regularly present your thoughts and temptations to God so he can purify you and guard you. Diligently offer your heart to God in prayer, and he will steer you into righteousness (Ps.139:23–24).

As you pray for your business, here are a few things to keep in mind:

First, guard your motives as you intercede for your business. Do you merely want God to make you rich and successful? God is not a genie in a lamp. He is God. You are his servant. It is ludicrous for you to act as if the reverse were true. The Lord will not listen to self-serving, temporal praying. He wants you to pray toward eternity. When James and John ambitiously petitioned Jesus for positions of influence, Jesus introduced them to the cross! (Mark 10:35–45). Similarly, if all your prayers are simply for your own prosperity, you are missing the point. Adjust your prayer life until you have a kingdom, God-honoring focus. As you pray for your company, offer your business to God for him to accomplish his purposes in his own way. Ask God to accomplish his will through the framework of your business ventures and client relationships. And be prepared to be amazed at how he responds!

Second, never forget that God's ways are not your ways (Isa. 55:8–9). The only hope for you to lead your organization in a Christlike manner is for Christ to lead *you.* You are no doubt a bright person, or you would not be in your position. But only God has eternal wisdom. You are beset with complex decisions as you seek to honor God in your work. Commonly accepted business practices are not always appropriate. In times of economic downturn, for example, cutbacks and layoffs are expected. But does God care more about the widow or the single parent than he does about profit margins? The most Christlike business approach may be to weather the storm and find other creative ways to cut costs so you preserve the well-being of employees. A merger with another company might make business sense, but if the other company's corporate practices would force you to compromise your own values; you are wise to refrain. Likewise, not every promotion is necessarily from God. Foolishly seeking and accepting every lucrative job offer without careful prayer can lead you into a lifestyle that is far from where God intended you to be.

In the Sermon on the Mount, Christ repeatedly said, "You have heard that it was said . . ." Then Jesus would give his own reciprocal perspective (Matt. 5:21, 27, 31, 33, 38, 43). When you face business situations, don't assume that what other business experts recommend is applicable to your situation. Rather, seek God's advice through prayer. God's answer for your organization may be radically different from what others are presently doing.

Third, Jesus instructed his disciples to pray, "Your kingdom come. Your will be done" (Matt. 6:10). This has aptly been called the prayer that never fails. God's kingdom ought to be the longing and focus of your prayers. Do not isolate your world as an entity unto itself. As an influence in the business world, you have a responsibility to seek the larger picture of where God is at work. Regularly praying for God's purposes will keep your view of your own business and career in its rightful perspective. Then you will see your job for what it is—a powerful instrument in God's hands.

Questions for Reflection

1. How have you usually prayed for your business?
2. What answers has God given to those prayers?
3. How might you intercede for your company and those who work there? Take note of the results as you pray for God's will in your company.

Additional Resources

Matthew 5:13–16; 38–42; 6:9–10, 31–33
Mark 9:23
Luke 5:16; 6:12; 11:9–10; 18:1; 21:36
Romans 8:26
1 Thessalonians 5:17

John D. Beckett, *Mastering Monday: A Guide to Integrating Faith and Work* (Downers Grove, IL: InterVarsity Press, 2006).
E. M. Bounds, *The Necessity of Prayer* (Springdale, PA: Whitaker House, 1984).

Dick Eastman, *The Hour that Changes the World: A Practical Plan for Personal Prayer* (Grand Rapids, MI: Baker Book House, 1978).
O. Hallesby, *Prayer* (Minneapolis: Augsburg Publishing House, 1931).
Andrew Murray, *With Christ in the School of Prayer* (Springdale, PA: Whitaker House, 1981).
Lloyd Reeb, *From Success to Significance: When the Pursuit of Success Isn't Enough* (Grand Rapids, MI: Zondervan, 2004).

How do I honor God when I have to fire someone and make other difficult business decisions?

Being a strong Christian does not mean you have to be a weak businessperson. In fact, people with integrity do not shy away from difficult decisions. The key factors are your motives and your methods. Is your impetus for downsizing or firing someone merely to increase profits? Is it to further your own career? God values people. He doesn't prize profits. If you are callously sending people to the unemployment lines so that quarterly earnings are closer to projections, don't expect God to be pleased with your actions. Scripture frequently cautions against allowing greed to motivate your behavior (1 Tim. 6:10; 1 John 2:15–17).

Along with every right *thing* to do is a right *way* to do it. It is possible for you to do the necessary thing but to dishonor God in your timing or in your methods. Businesses are not charities; sometimes costs must be cut to preserve the company. If you do not run your organization well, everyone, including you, will be out of work. So it is in your peoples' best interest for you to conduct your business prudently.

However, it is possible to run your establishment efficiently and still honor God. You may indeed be forced to let an employee go. We have both had that unpleasant experience. At times, employees prove to be incompetent, immoral, or disloyal. It becomes clear that they cannot be allowed to stay without jeopardizing the organization. But how you dismiss them will reveal whether you're a calloused businessperson or a spiritual statesperson. We are aware of business leaders who discharged someone so graciously that their former employee later thanked them.

Dismissal can sometimes provide a necessary and timely wake-up call for a person to reevaluate his or her motives and work ethic. Letting someone go can also motivate that individual to seek new and necessary skills to become more effective in the workplace. Some people naturally gravitate to the minimal work level required to keep their job. To retain such people on staff can dampen company morale and limit the business's success. Tolerating such behavior does no one any favors.

It's always important, though, to show kindness and generosity. Should you ever have to terminate someone's employment, seek to do so compassionately. It is not necessary to treat employees as if they have violated national security. Help preserve their dignity as much as possible. When appropriate, be as generous as you can with the severance package. Be sensitive to the financial hardships the person may face. Be gracious even when you have to be firm with employees. God wants your life to bless others. You want to reach the end of your business career with a legacy of integrity and generosity, despite the hard calls you had to make. People should feel grateful they worked for you. Some may even appreciate the candor with which you helped them meet the deficits in their character or work performance.

Before his famous Civil War accomplishments, Stonewall Jackson was a professor at the Virginia Military Institute. During his tenure there, he had a troublesome situation with a first classman, Cadet James A. Walker, who was scheduled to graduate in two months. Walker became belligerent toward his professor in class and refused to back down. Jackson ultimately had him court-martialed and expelled from the school. Walker was so outraged he threatened to kill Jackson. Ironically, Walker went on to become an attorney; and when the Civil War broke out, he was promoted to colonel and then brigadier general of the famous Stonewall Brigade. Long after Walker had cooled off, and thirty-nine years after his dismissal, Walker presided as the chief marshal over the unveiling of a monument to Stonewall Jackson in Lexington, Virginia. It is possible to make difficult decisions with integrity.

Questions for Reflection

1. Evaluate some of the difficult decisions you have had to enforce recently. Did your actions honor God?
2. How do you approach difficult dilemmas at work? Do you compartmentalize them as business decisions and conclude they are outside the spiritual domain? Or do you allow God to guide you?
3. What changes will you invite God to make in the way you handle difficult business situations?
4. Are there any actions you could take to rectify previous unchristlike business dealings?

Additional Resources

John D. Beckett, *Mastering Monday: A Guide to Integrating Faith and Work* (Downers Grove, IL: InterVarsity Press, 2006).

C. S. Lewis, *The Problem of Pain* (New York: Collier Books, 1962).

Does being a Christian change the way I develop strategies for my company and career?

If you are a leader in the world of business, finance, or politics, you wield significant influence, and you know it. You make plans; others carry them out. So it's hard to reverse this mentality when it comes to your relationship with God. But even the wealthiest, most powerful person on the planet is under God's sovereignty. This is simply the way it is. God is the master and judge of the universe. Servants do not instruct the master to do their bidding. And Christian leaders who do not acknowledge God's supremacy will never experience spiritual maturity. The basis for Christians' planning in any realm of life must be, "Our Father in heaven, Your name be honored as holy. Your kingdom come. Your will be done on earth as it is in heaven" (Matt. 6:9–10).

Effective leaders—Christians and non-Christians alike—plan for the future to avoid being caught unprepared by circumstances. Jesus, in fact, cautioned those who were considering following him:

Which of you, wanting to build a tower, doesn't first sit down and calculate the cost to see if he has enough to complete it? Otherwise, after he has laid the foundation and cannot finish it, all the onlookers will begin to make fun of him, saying, "This man started to build and wasn't able to finish." Or what king, going to war against another king, will not first sit down and decide if he is able with 10,000 to oppose the one who comes against him with 20,000? If not, while the other is still far off, he sends a delegation and asks for terms of peace. (Luke 14:28–32)

Jesus pointed out the folly of entering a venture while lacking the wherewithal to complete it. Our generation is both at an advantage and a disadvantage in this regard. Technology gives us fingertip access to current trends and projections, but it is evolving so rapidly that current knowledge quickly becomes obsolete. Prudent business leaders must prepare for an unpredictable future.

All business leaders must plan for the future in light of rapid and dynamic change. But the difference between a Christian businessperson and an unbeliever is the Holy Spirit who knows the Father's intentions. Jesus said the Spirit would guide Christians into truth regarding the future (John 16:13). He did not promise to reveal the future but to guide believers based on what God knows about the future (1 Cor. 2:9–16).

Christian businesspeople are to seek and follow the Holy Spirit's direction. Scripture calls it foolishness to plan apart from God. If we do so, should we be surprised when major developments (about which God was fully aware) thwart our plans? (Luke 12:16–21; James 4:13–16). An unforeseen event can render our best laid schemes irrelevant. Wise Christian leaders seek the Spirit of truth's guidance, for he has seen the future and can safely guide us into it.

What does it look like to plan under the Spirit's guidance? The key is prayer. Lay out your options before the Lord and remain receptive to any promptings his Word and the Spirit bring to your mind. The closer you walk with God, the more clearly you'll recognize where he is leading. Sometimes the path God points out will take you in a different direction than business pundits suggest. To follow God's way is not a sign of foolishness, however, but of obedience. Many Christian business leaders have weathered economic slumps during times when other companies downsized and spit out personnel. Yet God instructed them not to do so. They obeyed, and the ensuing year proved the wisdom of their actions. We know executives of one major corporation that, due to a downturn in the economy, faced a large operating deficit. Commonly accepted business logic was to initiate major layoffs. But several of the company's top leaders were Christians. They met and prayed together and sensed the Holy Spirit was guiding them to find other ways to cut the deficit. The Spirit guided them to cut millions of dollars out of operating expenses, and every job was preserved. Profits may not have been off the charts that year, but the executives' action induced renewed and tangible loyalty from employees.

Savvy business leaders use every tool at their disposal to plan and prepare for the future. These processes must be submitted to divine counsel, however, if they are to succeed and honor God. He will guide in specific and practical ways if you ask him. The Holy Spirit resides within you. Call upon him and allow him to guide you and your company into the future.

Questions for Reflection

1. How do you include God in your planning?
2. How has the Lord impacted your decision making?

Additional Resources

2 Chronicles 16:9

Psalm 111:2–3

Proverbs 1:28–33; 3:5–6; 4:23–27; 10:16; 10:24; 13:19; 14:12; 15:22; 16:33; 21:5; 21:31; 27:1; 29:18

Ecclesiastes 9:12
James 4:13–17
2 Peter 3:8

John D. Beckett, *Loving Monday: Succeeding in Business Without Selling Your Soul* (Downers Grove, IL: InterVarsity Press, 1998).

Henry Blackaby and Richard Blackaby, Claude King, *Experiencing God: Knowing and Doing the Will of God, Revised Edition* (Nashville: LifeWay Press, 2007).

Henry Blackaby and Richard Blackaby, *Hearing God's Voice* (Nashville: Broadman & Holman, 2002).

Henry Blackaby and Richard Blackaby, *Spiritual Leadership: Moving People on to God's Agenda* (Nashville: Broadman & Holman, 2001).

How should I respond when a colleague is trying to undermine me?

The corporate world operates aggressively. Everyone wants to succeed, and for some the surest way to the top is to eliminate the other contenders. Greed drives some beyond the boundary of business ethics. In the race to reach their goals, the power-hungry forsake healthy competition and go for the jugular. Survival of the fittest is their mantra. So how do Christians, guided by the divine command to love their enemies, operate in a world that fosters cutthroat competition? How are believers to respond when someone is surreptitiously discrediting them to satisfy their own career aspirations? Where does loving your enemies come in? Jesus said:

You have heard that it was said, "Love your neighbor" and hate your enemy. But I tell you, love your enemies and pray for those who persecute you, so that you may be sons of your Father in heaven. For He causes His sun to rise on the evil and the good, and sends rain on the righteous and the unrighteous. For if you love those who love you, what reward will you have? Don't even the tax collectors do the same? And if you greet only your brothers, what are you doing out of the ordinary? Don't even the Gentiles do the same? Be perfect, therefore, as your heavenly Father is perfect. (Matt. 5:43–48)

Loving an adversary is one of the most radical commands Jesus ever issued. It goes against our nature. We instinctively want to defend ourselves when someone attacks us. Why wouldn't we rush to protect our reputation when lies circulate about us? Jesus, however, set the standard when he prayed for the Father to forgive those who were brutally nailing him to a cross (Luke 23:34).

Imagine that an assertive young executive has recently joined your firm. He is already impressing management with his energy and ability. But he is also denigrating his colleagues to enhance his own standing. Now he is eyeing your position and has already aimed several darts at your job performance. You know he is actively critiquing your effectiveness in the company. How do you respond? Do you become indignant and fight fire with fire? What does God expect from you?

First, evaluate your own heart. Are you filled with anger? Do you long for revenge? Is your colleague's unethical behavior bringing out the worst in you? The way you respond to an enemy reveals the condition of your heart. Don't allow hostility to rob you of God's peace! Genesis 50:20 recounts that Joseph was betrayed by his own brothers, enticed by his boss's wife, maligned by his employer, and forgotten by his friend; yet he refused to become bitter. As a result, God honored Joseph and used his life to bless many people with an influence that extended down through many generations.

Second, you may need to correct falsehoods that have been spread about you, but be careful not to become obsessed with your reputation. God promised Samuel, "I will honor those who honor Me, but those who despise Me will be disgraced" (1 Sam. 2:30). When you begin following Christ, he takes responsibility for your reputation. People will not always respect you or treat you as you deserve, but let God defend you. Jesus himself was despised by many (Isa. 53:3), but ultimately God will vindicate him, and everyone will show him proper reverence (Phil. 2:10–11). You need not become absorbed by your own defense. The truth comes out eventually. Ask God to be your advocate and spend your energy guarding your own heart against sins such as anger and bitterness. Remaining silent or withholding retribution can be difficult, but God's presence in your life is a strong refuge against your enemies (Ps. 71).

Third, continue to live with Christlike integrity and let God's Spirit of truth sustain you. Loving your enemies and trusting God does not rule out being astute. Jesus instructed his disciples: "I'm sending you out like sheep among wolves. Therefore be as shrewd as serpents and as harmless as doves" (Matt. 10:16). Acting magnanimously does not make one a fool, but at the same time, allowing yourself to become an unnecessary martyr will not benefit anyone. Consider the case of Mordecai. When Mordecai discovered that the evil Haman intended to murder the Jewish people throughout the empire, he took immediate action to prevent this atrocity against innocent people. Mordecai judiciously allied himself with Queen Esther (Esther 4). The result was that Haman ultimately went to the gallows and Mordecai's position was exalted before the king (Esther 7, 10).

It is not God's will that his people be constantly trampled! But he does expect us to behave in a Christlike manner and to place our trust in him. God will guide you to know how to respond to your enemies. God always acts with grace and truth in perfect balance. Though he is long-suffering, gracious, and forgiving, he never compromises what is right. Jesus never forsook the truth, but he also forgave his oppressors even as they were murdering him. Likewise, God can guide you to stand up for truth while continuing to show grace toward those around you, even your enemies.

Fourth, consider whether a rival's attacks may be God's invitation for you to join him at work in that opponent's life. James 5:20 exhorts, "Whoever turns a sinner from the error of his way will save his life from death and cover a multitude of sins." We never know all the details of another person's life. Your antagonist's home life may be in shambles, or perhaps your colleague is under enormous financial strain. It could be that a dysfunctional upbringing left her thinking her value as a person is tied to her position in the organization. A coworker's attack on you could be God alerting you to this person's need. He could be envious of the peace and joy you demonstrate in your life. The one who maligns you might mistakenly assume your joy comes from your professional position rather than from your relationship to God. A conflict with someone could in fact be your opportunity to explain the source of your peace and confidence.

We know many Christian business leaders who were unfairly treated at work. On several occasions, the result was a lost job or a demotion. Yet these faithful Christians could also tell you marvelous stories of how he blessed them and how God used their example to provide a powerful testimony to others. At times, some of their harshest critics were deeply affected by their Christlike behavior. God is not concerned with how high you climb the corporate ladder; he is interested in how your life brings him glory. Suffering provides a unique opportunity to demonstrate that honoring Christ is more important to you than any corporate position or salary package.

If you are presently under attack by someone, turn to the Lord for strength. Read the Psalms. They are filled with the testimonies of those who suffered undeservedly. But most importantly, daily seek the Lord's will for this time in your life. Like the righteous man Job, your life may honor God in ways you do not presently understand. Stay true to your convictions, and experience God accomplishing his purposes through you.

Questions for Reflection

1. Do you have an enemy? What is he/she currently doing to you? How do you honestly feel about this person?
2. If you have grown bitter toward this individual, how has that affected the joy in your life?

3. What actions could you take in response to being mistreated that might alleviate the situation but also honor the Lord?
4. Which responses should you cease or avoid?
5. Has the Lord vindicated you when you were misrepresented? How has God previously defended your reputation? Do you trust him to do so again?

Additional Resources

Genesis 50:20

Psalm 1:6; 2:1–4; 3:1–3; 7:1; 9:9–10; 17:2; 18:1–2; 18:18; 20:7; 20:23; 25:20–21; 26:1; 26:11; 34:4; 34:18; 37:7; 37:23–25; 40:4; 41:11–12; 46:1; 55:22; 56:11

Isaiah 40:30; 48:10
Matthew 5:38–48
Philippians 1:15–18

Melvin Blackaby, *Going the Second Mile: Letting God Take You Beyond Yourself* (Sisters, OR: Multnomah, 2006).
Richard Blackaby, *Putting a Face on Grace: Living a Life Worth Passing On* (Sisters, OR: Multnomah, 2005).
Wes Cantrell and James R. Lucas, *High Performance Ethics: Ten Timeless Principles for Next Generation Leadership* (Carol Stream, IL: Tyndale House, 2007).

How do I guard myself from temptation?

People face numerous temptations every day (Rom. 1:28–32; 1 Cor. 6:9–10; Gal. 5:19–21; Col. 3:5–11; Titus 3:3), but the business world seems to intensify these enticements. The nature of the marketplace barrages the carnal senses: 1) success can foster pride and greed; 2) competition can test your ethics and breed jealousy; 3) gossip can spread like gangrene throughout the office; 4) sexual enticement is always close at hand. In such an environment, how can a Christian remain blameless? The apostle Paul answered that question:

> Whoever thinks he stands must be careful not to fall!
> No temptation has overtaken you except what is common
> to humanity. God is faithful and He will not allow you to be
> tempted beyond what you are able, but with the temptation
> He will also provide a way of escape, so that you are able to
> bear it. (1 Cor. 10:12–13).

Paul said to be realistic and to be ready. It is foolish to assume you are invulnerable. Have you known people who claimed they were impervious to certain temptations; then they fell victim to those very sins? Facing sin's lure is inevitable. Succumbing to temptation is not. The Bible assures us the Holy Spirit will give us strength to withstand any carnal bait the world dangles before us. The key is not our willpower; it's God's divine strength.

The Scriptures spell out our responsibility. Terms such as "guard your heart" appear over and over throughout Scripture. How foolish for a man to be cavalier in his interactions with female colleagues just because he thinks he's not prone to adultery! Likewise, a financial administrator should never neglect basic safeguards for the company funds because she thinks she is above tweaking the figures. Our pride can blind and disorient us to the imminent danger in front of us. The reality is that even if you don't go looking for temptation, it will come after you. Seduction can ambush you when and where you least expect it.

Understand that your temptations, though they may be many, are not unique. You are not the sole prey of the enemy. Everyone in every walk of life deals with pride, which is the basis of sin. Don't rationalize your sin by believing you have been somehow singularly targeted. Just as others have triumphed over the wiles of sin, you too have the Holy Spirit's promise of victory over whatever assaults you.

God watches over you and will help you in moments of weakness. Don't ever believe God has abandoned you to temptation. Wrongly assuming you are incapable of victory is in essence justifying your own sin and calling God a liar. God stands ready to deliver you, if you want to be rescued.

Immediately seize the opportunity to elude whatever temptation you face. God says an escape *will* be available. Of course you must take the escape route he provides. God will give you friends to hold you accountable, a church family to walk with you, the Holy Spirit to convict you, Scripture to guide you, family members to encourage you, Christian books to inform you, and countless other means of eluding your temptation; but you must use them! You are not powerless, but don't expect God to pluck you from danger. You must choose to flee. Potiphar's wife tried numerous tricks to seduce Joseph (Gen. 39:12), but Joseph chose the way of escape God provided him. He exited the scene as fast as his feet could carry him!

If you truly want to resist temptation, like Daniel you will make up your mind ahead of time that you *will not* defile yourself (Dan. 1:8). You will take practical steps to build a hedge of protection around yourself so you can avoid vulnerable positions. Be especially diligent when you are tired, traveling, isolated, or out of your normal routine. In these situations you may be particularly susceptible to sin. Prayer partners and accountability groups are extremely helpful in this regard. If you are married, share with your spouse what you are facing in your workplace, and pray together regularly.

Temptation is universal, but yielding to it is not a foregone conclusion. Jesus was tempted in all ways as we are, yet he never sinned (Heb. 4:15). Now your Savior seeks to live out his blameless life in you, and he is perfectly capable of achieving victory over the sin in *your* life, as well. Don't be overconfident about sin, but don't be intimidated by temptation either. The truth is, we are more than conquerors through him who loves us (Rom. 8:37).

Questions for Reflection

1. What temptations are intrinsic to your career?
2. How can you construct safeguards into your life to protect yourself in advance from temptation?
3. To whom are you presently accountable? How might you build more accountability into your life?
4. What way of escape has God provided for you in the face of specific temptations?

Additional Resources

1 Corinthians 10:12–13
2 Corinthians 5:17

Galatians 2:20
James 4:1–6
1 John 4:4

Henry Blackaby, *Holiness: God's Plan for Fullness of Life* (Nashville: Thomas Nelson, 2003).

Henry Blackaby, *Experiencing the Cross: Your Greatest Opportunity for Victory over Sin* (Sisters, OR: Multnomah, 2005).

Nancy Leigh DeMoss, *Holiness: The Heart God Purifies* (Chicago: Moody, 2004).

John Fischer, *On a Hill Too Far Away: Putting the Cross Back into the Center of Our Lives* (Minneapolis: Bethany House, 1994).

Beth Moore, *When Godly People Do Ungodly Things: Arming Yourself in the Age of Seduction* (Nashville: Broadman & Holman, 2002).

Deborah L. Rhode, ed., *Moral Leadership: The Theory and Practice of Power, Judgment, and Policy* (San Francisco: Jossey-Bass, 2006).

Charles H. Spurgeon, *Satan: A Defeated Foe* (Springdale, PA: Whitaker House, 1993).

How do I deal with a non-Christian boss or colleague whose actions and values are unethical?

For Christian businesspeople this is a serious matter because fundamentally, believers and unbelievers operate with entirely different paradigms. The apostle Paul advised:

> Do not be mismatched with unbelievers. For what partnership is there between righteousness and lawlessness? Or what fellowship does light have with darkness? What agreement does Christ have with Belial? Or what does a believer have in common with an unbeliever? And what agreement does God's sanctuary have with idols? (2 Cor. 6:14–16)

Believers and unbelievers are diametrically at odds on many issues. When a Christian and non-Christian join together in a marriage or business partnership, they invite disaster. If a Christian is under the influence or domination of an unbeliever, that situation is fraught with potential crisis. The safest path is to avoid entering partnerships with unbelievers.

However, it is not always possible to avoid working closely with non-Christians. While you *can* choose certain partnerships, it is not usually an option to conduct business only with Christians.

Here are a few points to consider: If your company forces you to violate your Christian values, you should seek other employment. We know many people who started their own business or moved to a smaller company so they could stay true to their Christian values. In the process, they endured a pay cut and slipped a rung or two on the corporate ladder, at least temporarily. But they honored God and retained their integrity. Likewise, when you are offered a promotion, first investigate the management of the new department. You may presently have a supportive boss who honors your personal and Christian commitments, but your new job may demand sacrifices you are unprepared to make. Some promotions are not worth the compromise demanded.

At times, you may have no choice in the matter. It is disheartening when an honest boss is replaced by one with less integrity. If your new supervisor is radically degrading your work environment or if you are pressured to do things that dishonor God or your family, drop to your knees and pray. Seek God's guidance for what to do. Perhaps God wants to use you as his instrument to set a carnal colleague free. Certainly God can teach you how to experience his joy and peace regardless of your present situation.

Don't be afraid to stand up for godly principles. If your boss is pressuring you to do some "creative accounting" in the company books, firmly refuse. Daniel believed no job was worth dishonoring God (Dan. 1:8; 6:10). He initially suffered for this conviction but was ultimately vindicated (Dan. 1:19–20; 6:28). When you refuse to compromise, your boss will either admire your spirit or else fire you. But it is far better to lose your job than your integrity. The Lord will not allow you to sacrifice for him without walking with you through the experience. Don't allow your career to hold you in bondage. Realize that Christ meant it when he said to seek *first* his kingdom, then he will give you everything else you need (Matt. 6:33).

God may want you to leave your current work situation for the sake of your family and your own spiritual health. Don't assume you must remain with your same company regardless of the circumstances. Salary level, health and retirement benefits, and job perks are not worth the risk of harming your marriage or conceding your Christian values. Some issues outweigh the usual measurements of job worth.

Above all, don't be intimidated. God has not given you a spirit of fear (2 Tim. 1:7). Christ who is in you is stronger than any evil force you may confront at work (1 John 4:4). Whether you are immersed in conflict with your boss, your board, or your business partner, when you take a stand for what is right, God will give you the words to say and the strength to follow through.

Evil abounds. It is impossible to avoid. God's people must be courageous in following their convictions, regardless of the outcome.

Questions for Reflection

1. Are you somehow unequally yoked at work? If so, how does the relationship affect you?
2. What are some ways you can ensure that your job does not compromise your Christian convictions?
3. Have you enlisted others to pray for you and your business relationships?
4. What fears may be holding you back from living out your faith in the business world? Losing clients? Losing your job? Losing a promotion? Being ridiculed? What has God told you about fear?

Additional Resources

Andrew Murray, *Like Christ* (Springdale, PA: Whitaker House, 1981).

Wes Cantrell and James R. Lucas, *High Performance Ethics: Ten Timeless Principles for Next Generation Leadership* (San Francisco: Jossey-Bass, 2007).

Charles Trumble, *Victory in Christ* (Whiting, NJ: The Sunday School Times Co., 1959).

How does being a Christian affect the way I respond to a crisis?

James instructed: "Consider it a great joy, my brothers, whenever you experience various trials, knowing that the testing of your faith produces endurance. But endurance must do its complete work, so that you may be mature and complete, lacking nothing" (James 1:2–4).

A crisis is an opportunity for God to reveal his nature and power through believers to a watching world. Everyone faces moments of helplessness. But in seasons like these, Christians should instinctively turn to God, whether the problem is personal or business. Our immediate dependence on God strengthens our relationship with him. It can also transmit a potent message to non-Christian colleagues.

James reminds us that in the midst of life's exigent circumstances, all we have to do is ask God for the wisdom we need (James 1:5). Peter adds: "You rejoice in this, though now for a short time you have had to be distressed by various trials so that the genuineness of your faith—more valuable than gold, which perishes though refined by fire—may result in praise, glory, and honor at the revelation of Jesus Christ" (1 Pet. 1:6–7).

Christian history bears extensive witness to God's people finding themselves in precarious circumstances. Yet history also testifies that

Christians have boldly overcome adversity by trusting God. If you are at a critical juncture in your workplace, remember to count it all joy that God is choosing to use your faith (your confident hope in God) to reveal himself to you, to your family, and to those around you (James 1:2).

Potential calamities threaten the business world daily. The media reminds us of this reality by spectacularizing economic and political events. Executives can tend to be worriers. Business leaders carry enormous responsibility, and a wrong decision on their part can lead to extensive loss for others. So how should a believer respond to the quandaries of corporate life?

First, keep your heart, mind, and spirit focused on God. A crisis is not the time to be too busy to pray or read your Bible. Keep sight of Almighty God on his throne, and act accordingly from that vantage point. Isaiah feared the inevitable political and economic instability that the death of King Uzziah would precipitate. At this tumultuous juncture, Isaiah "saw the Lord seated on a high and lofty throne" (Isa. 6:1). After seeing God, Isaiah's concerns no longer focused on political ramifications but on God and his activity.

Second, approach the dilemma with a long-term perspective. Leaders often panic in the face of events that could resolve themselves over time. History is a great teacher. It reveals that many situations are not nearly as critical as they first appear. In Isaiah's case, his nation trembled at the intimidating power of the Assyrian Empire. The Assyrians at that time were the world's superpower, and they were a menacing enemy. Yet God assured Isaiah:

> The Lord GOD of Hosts says this: "My people, who dwell in Zion, do not fear Assyria, though he strikes you with a rod and raises his staff over you as the Egyptians did. In just a little while My wrath will be spent and My anger will turn to their destruction."

And the LORD of Hosts will brandish a whip against him
as He did when He struck Midian at the rock of Oreb; and He
will raise His staff over the sea, as He did in Egypt. On that
day his burden will fall from your shoulder, and his yoke from
your neck. The yoke will be broken because of his fatness.
(Isa. 10:24–27)

God reassured his servant Isaiah that despite how ominous the mighty
Assyrians appeared, they would be obliterated. Likewise, God knows the
future of your company, the economy, and your career. Don't be like the
disciples who panicked in the storm when Christ himself was in their boat
(Luke 8:22–25). Does this mean the threats are not real? No, it indicates
that now is the time to call on the Lord in the middle of the tempest.

*Third, allow God's peace to permeate your life so that even the worst
situations do not rob you of the joy of the Lord.* Scripture says God's peace
can put a sentry around your heart and mind so that nothing shakes you
(Phil. 4:6–7). Christians ought to bring God's peace to a troubled workplace. Others can look to believers for courage and assurance because
Christians know the source of peace. Ask God for calm and confidence
even when everything seems to be falling apart. Christian employees often
reach high levels of responsibility because of the confident way they handle
adversity.

Why does God allow crises in our world? When times are prosperous
and life is clear sailing, people (even Christians) can assume they are self-
sufficient. When storms hit, we realize how inadequate we are to face life's
challenges. We pray more during turbulent times. Perhaps God will get the
attention of people in your workplace by allowing a crisis and using you to
model what it means to trust God in every circumstance.

Christians aren't naïve. We know problems will come. But unlike
unbelievers, Christians should be ready to experience victory in the midst
of whatever life brings.

Questions for Reflection

1. Are you presently facing a crisis? If so, what is it?
2. How would you evaluate the way you generally handle adversity? Is God honored by the way you respond to a crisis?
3. How can you change the way you handle setbacks to better reflect your faith in God? What steps will you take to make this happen?

Additional Resources

2 Chronicles 16:9
Psalms 20:7; 20:23; 34:19; 37:39–40; 40:1–5; 56:4; 56:71; 91:1–2
Isaiah 41:10
Jeremiah 33:3
Matthew 11:28–30
Romans 8:31–39

Henry Blackaby and Richard Blackaby, *Hearing God's Voice* (Nashville: Broadman & Holman, 2002).
John Hunter, *Knowing God's Secrets* (Grand Rapids, MI: Zondervan, 1965; Renewed ed., Kingsport, TN: Fresh Springs Publications, 1995).
Charles Trumble, *Victory in Christ* (Whiting, NJ: The Sunday School Times Co., 1959).

How can I be less political and more spiritually driven in my work?

Have you noticed that politicians often approach problems and issues from a popular perspective rather than a moral viewpoint? They say what the public wants to hear. Unfortunately, public servants' motivation to act often comes from the need to gain votes and to discredit the opposition. Politicians often vociferously denounce questionable conduct by their rivals but turn a blind eye to the same behavior in their own lives. This double standard is what makes people lose confidence in politicians.

Likewise, business leaders often base their decisions on political considerations. A healthy profit can drive business leaders to excuse the harm their company is causing the environment. Executives sometimes set aside their own personal principles just long enough to gain a promotion or to receive recognition within their company. Leaders can massage the truth to divert blame for a company's failure while readily accepting the credit for its success. In pursuing profit, some managers mistreat and exploit employees. Staff may be underpaid, overworked, or callously laid off in the relentless quest to satisfy shareholders. People of shallow character can nevertheless be praised in business circles as organizational gurus and political geniuses.

What our world needs more than business superstars are spiritual statesmen—men and women who rise above the pursuit of their personal agendas to lead people and organizations to please and honor God.

Here are eight characteristics of such leaders:

1. *A spiritual statesperson honors God.* First and foremost, spiritual statesmen prioritize honoring God over pleasing people. First Samuel 2:35 says, "Then I will raise up a faithful priest for Myself. He will do whatever is in My heart and mind." Spiritual statespersons are men and women who have the heart and mind of God. They invest their lives in the things God values. They seek to honor God despite the constant temptation to impress people. A related verse is 1 Samuel 2:30, where God says, "I will honor those who honor Me, but those who despise Me will be disgraced." Honoring God means trusting your reputation to him, living so that *he* will be pleased with you when you eventually give an account to him for your life (2 Cor. 5:9–10).

William Wilberforce is an example of this moral courage. Forfeiting a promising possibility of becoming Britain's prime minister, he embraced instead the most unpopular issue of his day—slavery. He never won that coveted political office, but God used him to change his world.

We work with men and women who are Christian leaders in corporate America. They strive to conduct their business careers in a godly manner. Some have been called to take moral stands that have cost them promotions or even their jobs. God has led some to pray in their boardroom or to lead Bible studies for their employees, even though they knew criticism or hostility might result. Some of these business leaders have knowingly forfeited opportunities for career advancement by refusing to compromise their beliefs. Instead they have boldly spoken out for their biblical principles. Many brilliant and creative people have been maligned and slandered in the press because of their faith. Being a committed Christian is not easy, especially in the corporate world; but one cannot honor God and simultaneously compromise his Word.

2. A spiritual statesperson embodies integrity. Integrity prevails in all that a spiritual statesman does. Noah's life provides a poignant example. Genesis 6:9 describes him this way: "Noah was a righteous man, blameless among his contemporaries, Noah walked with God." What an honorable biography! According to the standard of Noah's day, no fault could be found in him.

Likewise, when Samuel approached the end of his leadership tenure, he stood before his people to give an account, for he had lived among them his entire life. This is what Samuel said:

> "Here I am. Bring charges against me before the LORD and His anointed: Whose ox or donkey have I taken? Whom have I wronged or mistreated? From whose hand have I taken a bribe to overlook something? I will return it to you."
>
> "You haven't wronged us, you haven't mistreated us, and you haven't taken anything from anyone's hand," they responded.
>
> He said to them, "The LORD is a witness against you, and His anointed is a witness today that you haven't found anything in my hand."
>
> "He is a witness," they said. (1 Sam. 12:3–5)

After years under his godly leadership, the people unanimously confirmed Samuel's sterling integrity. What an inspiring legacy.

Integrity means more than talking a good talk or maintaining a shiny public image. It signifies that people remain blameless despite the most thorough investigation of their words and actions. Sadly, people in our day often look in vain for integrity in their leaders.

People with integrity can withstand intense scrutiny because they have nothing to hide. They are the same in private as they are in public. It takes years to earn a reputation of integrity but only a few careless moments to destroy it. Business leaders with integrity can boldly pledge along with Job, "I will maintain my integrity until I die" (Job 27:5).

3. *A spiritual statesperson embraces truth.* God expects his people to speak the truth regardless of whether it is popular. Godly leaders do not play games with semantics. Their words are not hollow rhetoric; they have substance that can be validated. They put away falsehood (Eph. 4:25). Statesmen do not hedge their words and hide behind double meanings. What they say is what they mean.

4. *A spiritual statesperson does things God's way.* There is a right thing to do and also a right way to do it. God's ways are not our ways (Isa. 55:8–9). Statesmen seek to understand God's methods (Ps. 25:4–5; 27:11). God doesn't take shortcuts; he cares about the process. He builds upon what he has already done. God finishes what he starts and he leaves no loose ends. Institutions, buildings, budgets, and programs will pass away, but people are eternal; and they are God's priority. God is holy. Everything God does on earth is for the purpose of bringing people to himself. God's activity is completely consistent with his nature. Spiritually astute men and women seek to honor God by doing the right things God's way.

It can be sorely tempting to compromise the means in order to achieve certain ends. Many CEOs have experienced spectacular falls into illegal activity and eventual prosecution, but they did not begin their careers planning to break the law. They often started out with the best of intentions. Then they yielded to the temptation to cut corners and to tell partial truths. Once compromise began, it inevitably led to more concessions until there seemed no turning back. That is always sin's pattern. The first lie may be a small one, but it charts the course for a destructive journey.

5. *A spiritual statesperson glorifies God.* Spiritual statespeople exalt God by their actions (1 Cor. 10:31; Col. 3:17). Pastors and missionaries are not the only people who should exalt God through their daily work. Christian business leaders are also called to glorify God, and they must live accordingly.

Our good friend John Beckett, chairman of R. W. Beckett Corporation in Elyria, Ohio, seeks to honor God daily through his business behavior. His leadership over his company is so unusual by worldly standards that ABC News sent a team to interview him. During the evening network news, John was asked to share his life goal. Without hesitation he declared, "To know and do the will of God."

Sadly, the world does not admire pastors and religious leaders the same way it once did. Today's heroes are often successful businesspeople. But one upside of this shift is worth noting: you as a businessperson have a tremendous platform today for exalting the Savior.

6. *A spiritual statesperson is trustworthy.* They steadfastly build a track record that invites trust. They keep their promises and consistently live out their faith, demonstrating through their relationships that people can count on them.

There are no shortcuts to building a track record.

Every year, some athletes go through periods where they temporarily play at a level that is above average in their sport. It could be in home runs or scoring goals or breaking records. Sportscasters spot the trend and give daily updates on the athlete's superior accomplishments. Yet a winning streak does not ensure the athlete's admittance into a hall of fame. That requires consistency over the long haul. Statesmen are not people who rise up in a moment and make a dramatic speech or perform one heroic action. They steadily—over time—do the right thing. They are considered trustworthy because they have proven themselves year in and year out.

7. *A spiritual statesperson demonstrates wisdom.* Statesmen see the big picture when others are distracted and consumed by current issues. God's people should not be swayed by temporary fads but guided by timeless principles. They discern between what is important and what is trivial. They know God's Word, and they recognize how Scripture applies to their situation. They build their lives and careers on the Bible so life's inevitable trials cannot shake them (Matt. 7:24–27).

These are the leaders to whom people inevitably turn during crises, the ones they seek out for advice. Their own lives manifest the wisdom they share with others. The Psalms describe them as fertile trees that provide shelter and sustenance to those around them (Ps. 1:1–3). There will always be occasions when statespersons are criticized and ridiculed, but time will prove the wisdom of their actions (Luke 7:35).

Statesmanship has always been a sensitive area for U.S. presidents. Harry Truman stood by convictions that were highly unpopular on certain issues. As a result, he left office with one of the lowest presidential approval ratings in American history. Yet decades later he is consistently rated among the top American presidents. Truman sought to do what he understood to be right, and history has demonstrated the wisdom of many of his decisions. Lesser leaders have sought public approval for the moment, and they forfeited becoming statesmen as a result.

8. *A spiritual statesperson is motivated by God's will.* Business leaders are obviously not averse to making a profit. But that should not be the chief motivation of their lives. Corporate success or personal wealth will not accompany anyone into eternity. Investing in people and doing God's will is characteristic of a godly leader.

Many Christian business leaders are more generous to their employees than the industry norm dictates. Their benevolence is not just good business; they feel a stewardship of their employees. We know CEOs who invest company resources into providing generous maternity benefits or college scholarships or skills upgrading for their employees. We also know business owners who roll a large percentage of their profits back into the community or into their church and mission projects. These business leaders are not driven by the compelling need to make more and more money. As a result they are free to use their businesses to further God's kingdom and to enhance the lives of their employees.

The world desperately needs spiritual statesmen in the marketplace. Businesspeople can often do what preachers and missionaries cannot. Isn't it interesting that when Jesus chose twelve disciples he found them in the marketplace? He chose a dozen businessmen. These men had a lot to learn about the kingdom of God, but they knew the world and how to operate in it. Similarly, several of the early church leaders were businesspeople, including Lydia, Aquilla and Priscilla, and Joseph of Arimathea.

Today's businesspeople understand how the world functions—they have to in order to succeed in their jobs. They have contacts throughout the marketplace. Their network among other Christians crosses denominational lines.

If God were to bring sweeping revival today, it might not come through a church. Many denominations are isolated, and a revival in one group of churches might never reach other Christian organizations. Revival could, however, come through the marketplace. Christian businesspeople are connected though multiple denominations. The business community by nature is oriented toward results. Many Christian businesspeople are wary of theological hairsplitting, and they are bewildered by the adamant refusal of church leaders to cooperate with one another. In the marketplace, networking and pooling resources make sense.

Christian business leaders must refuse to be self-centered, politicizing profiteers. Instead they must allow God to elevate their lives and their leadership to that of statespersons. God did that with a handful of fishermen and local business leaders in the first century, and the world continues to feel the impact. God can do it again today. Are you willing to allow God to make you a statesperson for your generation?

Questions for Reflection

1. Do you act like a politician, or like a statesman? Explain.
2. What evidence is there that you seek to please God above everyone else?
3. Are you wholly committed to the truth at all costs?

4. How have you been sensitive to the means by which you reach your goals? Are they as important to you as the ends you are striving to achieve?
5. How would you rate your integrity? Would others agree with your self-assessment?
6. How has God been glorified lately through your business activity?
7. Do others view you as trustworthy? Has that been your track record?

Additional Resources

1 Kings 9:4
Psalm 7:8; 25:21; 26:1; 26:11; 41:11–12
Matthew 6:33
Acts 4:19–20
1 Corinthians 1:25; 3:21
Galatians 1:10
Ephesians 4:25
Colossians 3:17
1 Thessalonians 2:4

Henry Blackaby and Roy Edgemon, *The Ways of God: How God Reveals Himself Before a Watching World* (Nashville: Broadman & Holman, 2000).

Ken Blanchard, *It Takes Less than One Minute to Suit up for the Lord* (Mechanicsburg, PA: Executive Books, 2004).

John Beckett, *Loving Monday: Succeeding in Business Without Selling Your Soul* (Downers Grove, IL: InterVarsity Press, 1998).

John Beckett, *Mastering Monday: A Guide to Integrating Faith and Work* (Downer's Grove: InterVarsity Press, 2006).

Regi Campbell, *About My Father's Business: Taking Your Faith to Work* (Sisters, OR: Multnomah, 2005).

Wes Cantrell and James R. Lucas, *High Performance Ethics: Ten Timeless Principles for Next-Generation Leadership* (San Francisco: Jossey-Bass, 2007).

Eric Metaxas, *Amazing Grace: William Wilberforce and the Heroic Campaign to End Slavery* (San Francisco: Harper Collins, 2007).

Truett S. Cathy, *It's Easier to Succeed than to Fail* (Nashville: Oliver Nelson, 1989).

How do I know when it is time to leave my present job?

Barring the appearance of a pink slip on your desk, it can be much harder to decide whether to leave a job than to accept one. There are two sides to the coin. Perhaps you're extremely unhappy at work, but you don't want to bail out. Or maybe you love your job, but you sense God calling you to a new challenge or to retire. Here are a few things to keep in mind:

First, God is concerned with every stage of your life. If you sense a stirring in your heart, pay attention. God may have a new assignment for you. Never become so complacent or comfortable that you are not receptive to a new challenge from God.

Second, realize that your value and self-worth do not come from a career or position but from your relationship with God. Jobs are temporary and do not follow you into the next life. There is only one CEO in heaven! This knowledge frees you from clinging to a job at all costs as though your personal worth depended on it.

Third, God has a purpose for everything he asks of you. He led you to your current job with specific plans for your tenure. So when you consider leaving your present position, you should evaluate more than merely what a new job might offer. Ask yourself if you have accomplished what God called you to do in your current position. We have both received various job offers throughout the years. Many of these opportunities included higher pay and more benefits, but that should not be the driving force in a career decision. We always asked ourselves, "Have I completed my assignment here?" When Jesus hung on the cross, he had conducted a brief public ministry of less than four years. Yet he triumphantly shouted, "It is finished!" (John 19:30). At times, businesspeople get their organization into disastrous condition; then, rather than cleaning up their mess, they grasp the next opportunity that comes along and flee the scene. This is a dereliction of duty. The success of a career is not measured by how long it lasts or by how many material possessions were attained; what matters is whether God's divine assignment was accomplished.

Fourth, there will be indicators that it is time for you to move on to a new assignment. Business may be flourishing, and yet you feel restless and unsettled, eager for a fresh challenge. This could mean you were faithful in what God called you to do, and now he is preparing you for something different (Matt. 25:21). God may no longer be giving you a vision for your company. Perhaps God is gently detaching you from your current company so you can be ready for a career move. Other signs could come from the people you lead. Perhaps someone in the ranks could effectively replace you. Having a qualified successor could free you up to undertake a new opportunity. If the people you lead are beginning to chafe under your leadership, consider whether you have led them as far as you can. Is it time for a leader with different skills to take the organization to the next level? God will let you know when your tenure in your present job is drawing to a close. The question is whether you will accept or ignore the signs. Don't fall into the trap of thinking you are indispensable. God can raise up a leader for any job.

Finally, remember that God is never through with you! He always has another assignment. Henry's father-in-law, Melvin Wells, recently passed away at the age of ninety-six. He had been a successful salesman for decades. When he retired from that job, he and his wife Carrie immediately departed for Africa to care for missionary children. It was the happiest period of their lives. When they returned to the U.S. several years later, Melvin took on a temporary position for a major newspaper, convincing people who had cancelled their subscription to re-subscribe. He was so good at it (a natural salesman), they had him make a demo tape to show the younger employees how to do it. Then Melvin took a job as a state representative for a large organization representing senior adults, traveling back and forth to the state capital for meetings. He also volunteered to visit people in the hospital each week. Well into his eighties, he purchased his first computer so he could keep up with all of his correspondence! Here was a man who never quit a job merely to enjoy idle time; rather, he was constantly transitioning from one assignment to the next as the Lord guided him.

Could God be preparing you for a job change or even a whole new career? Is he calling you out of the business world to devote your life to full-time Christian ministry? Diligently seek him and allow him to guide you. Walking with God makes life a continuing adventure. He always has a fresh new assignment waiting for you when you have been faithful with your previous one. Seek counsel from wise Christians and prayerfully consider whether a move is in your future.

Questions for Reflection

1. Do you sense God may be leading you to change jobs? If so, what are the signs?
2. Have you accomplished, to the best of your ability, the major work God called you to complete at your current job?
3. Are there signs you have stayed too long in your present job? If so, what is holding you there?

Additional Resources

Genesis 12:1
Exodus 3:1–10
Joshua 14:6–12
Psalm 37:18, 23
Matthew 9:9
Mark 1:16–20

Henry Blackaby and Richard Blackaby, Claude King, *Experiencing God: Knowing and Doing the Will of God, Revised Edition* (Nashville: LifeWay Press, 2007).

Henry Blackaby and Richard Blackaby, *Hearing God's Voice* (Nashville: Broadman & Holman, 2002).

Andrew Murray, *God's Plans for You* (New Kensington, PA: Whitaker House, 1983).

Larry Collett
Chairman and Chief Executive Officer
Cass Information Systems

While the role of CEO in a publicly owned company demands many areas of focus, I believe one of the key principles to remember is that the economy is really under God's control.

CEOs are paid to provide direction and to make things happen that result in increasing value—to shareholders, to employees, to the community, and to customers and suppliers. If CEOs believe they can make this happen through their own ability, they are deceiving themselves and are being set up for a huge disappointment. Even the best visions, plans, and strategies can be upset or discarded because of changes that occur beyond the control of corporate management. When that happens, the CEO is usually discarded as well!

In addition, any attempts by CEOs to manage or control the external environment are sure to meet with even less success. Politics, law, education, social structures, weather, and the like all have a way of influencing activity at times and degrees that can cause turmoil in the business environment. Even the best of Federal Reserve chairmen are unable to avoid such disruptions.

If we believe that God is omnipotent—and I believe we must if we are ever to really trust him—then we must recognize that he is also in control of the world's economies. The implications of this are huge! Initially, it means that all aspects of our leadership are only as good as he allows them to be. Secondly, it means our definition of success will appear much different than the world's perspective. And finally, it means the way we manage our businesses and personal lives will be significantly impacted.

There are some insights into how this occurs. The first is that we must be in constant communication with him. We all recognize how critical it is to communicate with our board of directors, shareholders, managers, and staff. But spending time with the One ultimately in control is far more imperative. Why try to take a direction or activity that may be contrary to what he desires?

Next, in order to communicate with him, we clearly must believe that he will respond. Waiting for that response, recognizing it, and moving in a consistent direction then becomes mandatory. Keeping a record is also important. With all the activities and time demands on a CEO, it is easy to forget.

We also recognize that given the statutory and market demands on a CEO, we are called to an even higher level of success. In fact, our whole perspective on wealth and success changes as we put our trust in God's leadership. We realize that we need to seek spiritual riches far more than tangible ones—eternal treasures that will not erode or dissipate like last year's profit results. Clearly, we are called to a more long-term perspective. Not recognizing the call of God on our business is to disassociate what we're doing from the will of the One who is ultimately in charge. After all, a CEO would never intentionally act contrary to the directives of his board or regulators, realizing that this would clearly invite negative consequences. Why is it any different with God?

Additionally, we are called to turn our thinking (including our logic) completely over to God. This is a difficult discipline for a CEO to grasp. Indeed, one of the key reasons why people become CEOs is because of their ability to think rationally, cogently, and factually. God certainly doesn't ask us to discontinue such thinking. But he does ask us to turn over the conclusions or results of our thinking to him before we begin to execute.

One of the biggest mistakes I made in past years was to assume God was always present in my logic and, therefore, he would always approve of the results. While I may have brought him into the process, my conclusions were never turned over to him for final evaluation and insight. As a result, many of the decisions were mine alone. In reality, I was asking God to endorse my plan of action rather than seeking his. While he obviously blessed our company, I am sure he wanted to perform even greater things. The kingdom's economy always produces much greater and lasting benefits than the world's.

The role of a CEO can be an exciting and awesome adventure. Too often, however, we are occupied with managing potential risks rather than being led into new and uncharted territory. In many ways, the CEO is similar to an ambassador of the State Department. These positions require the incumbent to represent our country in a foreign land, but they are to get their orders and instructions from their home officials. If we are in proper alignment with God, we also are getting our instructions from the One in charge. We, too, are ambassadors in a foreign land, representing the leader of the only kingdom that will last. He thinks much differently than us worldly creatures—at a much higher level—producing far greater growth, dynamics, continuity, and results than we could ever envision.

Who's in charge out there? I'm sure we often ask that question as we engage the external and internal business environments. Too often we conclude it is out of control. It isn't! Our charge is to stay in touch with and follow the leader. After all, it's his economy!

LARRY COLLETT is chairman and CEO of Cass Information Systems, Inc., the largest provider of outsourced freight and utility payment services in North America, processing more than $20 billion annually. He was recently named one of the nation's best CEOs by DeMarche Associates, a Kansas City-based consulting company. *Forbes* magazine designated Cass as one of the nation's top small public companies. It is also a member of the Russell 2000, a well-recognized list of public companies selected for inclusion in this highly respected investment fund. Larry has held numerous positions with civic, charitable, and church-related groups, chairing numerous fund raising activities for non-profit and educational institutions in the St. Louis area. He and his wife, Sharon, have three children and six grandchildren.

PART 3

My Devotional Life

A relationship with Jesus Christ is the most important thing in a Christian's life. We're not just saying it *should* be so or that you should try to *make* it so. The reality is that your walk with God, however close or distant, deep or shallow, will dramatically affect your entire life whether you acknowledge it or not.

People often assume that any Christian businessperson who could build a Fortune 500 company must also have a dynamic walk with God. Thus, business leaders often quickly gain the confidence of their fellow church members. Local churches and Christian organizations routinely place them on prominent boards and in influential leadership positions. In reality, many business leaders privately grieve over the fact they have invested the best years of their life making themselves and their companies successful while concurrently neglecting their own spiritual life.

Jesus said: "Seek first the kingdom of God and His righteousness, and all these things will be provided for you" (Matt. 6:33). What are "all these things"? They could include a spouse, a home, a good reputation, an impressive collection of "stuff," children, and so on. Jesus was not denying the joy and contentment that such things bring. He was emphasizing the urgent need of putting God first. Jesus assured his disciples that the Father knew their needs (Matt. 6:25–26). When you delight yourself in the Lord, he provides everything you require to have a joy-filled life (Ps. 37:4).

Christians generally acknowledge that the most important aspect of their lives is their walk with God (Deut. 30:11–20). Yet they allow the responsibilities of daily life to crowd out and subordinate their intimate relationship with Christ. In sidelining this most crucial pursuit, they inevitably settle for less than the abundant life Christ promises (John 10:10). One's devotional life is not merely religious practices and disciplines; it is the heart of the believer's life (Deut. 32:44–47).

Little children often equate going to church with having a relationship with Jesus. They eventually learn that the former is a response to the latter. But somewhere along the way, overworked, overwhelmed adults revert to this childish fallacy: I go to church; therefore, I have a relationship with God.

Joining a church, attending services, volunteering on committees—none of these makes you a mature Christian. Such activity does, however, produce results. Most business leaders we know are intelligent and creative people. When they channel their powerful abilities into supporting their church, the results can be impressive. But at what cost? The church as an organization benefits, but these leaders may have diverted their energy at the expense of their relationship with God.

We have talked with perplexed businesspeople who longed for their walk with God to be all it could be. But their job and their church placed so many demands on them, they lost sight of the main thing. If these same people used their ingenuity, vitality, and resolve to pursue a deeper walk with God, they would experience amazing spiritual growth. Here are some of the questions we often hear from businesspeople who are seeking a more intimate relationship with the Lord.

How can I know God's will for my life?

This is by far the question we hear most often. Most people want to invest their lives wisely. Christians don't want to spend their best years merely pursuing their own goals and in the process bypass God's will. Yet they have trouble discerning exactly what God's plan is.

But however compelling this question is, it is flawed because it is fundamentally self-centered. A healthy relationship with God must be God-centered. Consider Moses' life. Moses grew up in Pharaoh's court in Egypt, yet he was keenly aware of his people's oppression. While Moses enjoyed the opulence of Egyptian nobility, he watched his countrymen toiling as slaves under their cruel Egyptian taskmasters. Moses may have wondered, "Lord, why did you rescue me from slavery? Why do I enjoy such comfort while my people suffer so grievously? What can I do to ease their burdens? How do I deal with the guilt I feel for not helping my family when I have so much and they have so little?"

Ultimately, Moses was overcome by the burden to help the oppressed Israelites and, taking matters into his own hands, he committed murder (Exod. 2:11–12). Moses' best intentions transformed him into a fugitive for the next forty years. His focus was primarily upon himself and what he could do to rescue his family and friends. God had no part in his plans. That thinking led to disaster.

Then one day Moses had an encounter with God. God did not ask him what his dreams for the future were. God didn't ask Moses for his personal life goals or to list his spiritual gifts. God didn't need Moses to report on the oppressed condition of the Hebrew people. God told Moses what *he* was about to do:

> The LORD said, "I have observed the misery of My people in Egypt, and have heard them crying out because of their oppressors, and I know about their sufferings. I have come down to rescue them from the power of the Egyptians and to bring them from that land to a good and spacious land, a land flowing with milk and honey—the territory of the Canaanites, Hittites, Amorites, Perizzites, Hivites, and Jebusites. The Israelites' cry for help has come to Me, and I have also seen the way the Egyptians are oppressing them." (Exod. 3:7–9)

For the first time, Moses heard God's agenda. And the Lord's plans far surpassed anything Moses could have conjured up. Moses only wanted to alleviate the Hebrews' suffering and to improve the worst of their working conditions. God was going to free the nation completely, give them their own prosperous land, and bless all the nations of the earth through them. So God had a specific invitation for Moses: "Therefore, go. I am sending you to Pharaoh so that you may lead My people, the Israelites, out of Egypt" (Exod. 3:10).

This was huge! Once Moses heard what *God* was doing, everything else in Moses' life made sense. Now he knew why God saved him as a baby from certain death. Now he understood his deep burden for the oppression of his people. Now Moses could see the folly of his earlier attempt to rescue one of his countrymen. God was about to orchestrate something on a scale far beyond what Moses could have done, and God was inviting him to join him in this miraculous venture.

For the rest of Moses' life, he focused on God and his plans. Moses watched for God's activity and then responded when God invited him to join him in his work. At the close of Moses' life, people did not marvel at Moses' excellent career choices. No one praised Moses for discovering his gifts and developing a ministry for God. Everyone glorified God. God had taken an ordinary person and done extraordinary things through him.

A self-centered viewpoint obstructs our ability to hear from God. If believers will become intimately acquainted with God and his activity around them rather than spending their prayer times asking God to bless their efforts, they will begin to understand God's heart. Then they can become involved in what God intends to accomplish. The difference between the questions "What is God's will for my life?" and "What is God's will?" is not just semantics; it is a radically different approach to viewing life and walking with God.

As Jesus was entering Jerusalem to attend a feast, he approached a multitude of sick people, all clamoring to be healed. The situation must have been overwhelming; the crowd deafening. How disconcerting to be surrounded by so much need! But Jesus turned aside and healed only one person, a man who had been lame for thirty-eight years (John 5:1–8). When asked why he zeroed in on one person, Jesus responded:

> I assure you: The Son is not able to do anything on His own, but only what He sees the Father doing. For whatever the Father does, the Son also does these things in the same way. For the Father loves the Son and shows Him everything He is doing, and He will show Him greater works than these so that you will be amazed. (John 5:19–20)

Jesus might have been tempted to bypass the crowd to hurry to his appointment. Or he might have chosen to tarry and heal everyone. But he knew his Father well and immediately recognized him working in that solitary life. So he responded specifically to his Father's activity. Jesus didn't question why he shouldn't heal all the others; he trusted the Father to make that choice.

Even when the Father's will was difficult, Jesus yielded wholeheartedly (Matt. 26:39, 42). The key is first recognizing that we are God's servants; God does not serve us. God's purpose is not to grant all our prayer requests and to make us happy. We are God's attendants. We wait for him to reveal his will, and then we respond in obedience. When we resolutely seek God's directives with a predisposition to obedience, God is pleased to reveal his will to us. And usually his plans don't look anything like what we anticipated.

Seeking to know God's will and adjusting your life to it looks different from developing your own action plan. Here are several guidelines for discerning God's will in any situation:

First, plan in advance to respond in obedience. There is no point in seeking God's will if you are not committed to obey it (Luke 6:46).

Second, be prepared to wait. Moses had to wait forty years before he learned God's will for his people.

Third, focus on God and his activity in the world around you. This will place your own issues and concerns in perspective. We are predisposed to be self-centered and to assume God is orchestrating the entire planet to meet our needs. God always relates to us in the context of his concern to redeem a lost world.

Fourth, set your preconceptions and preferences aside so you are receptive to what God says. Don't try to force God into your plans to accomplish your goals. Don't limit yourself by trying to identify some spiritual gift or appealing career path. Rather, open your life completely to the great work he intends to accomplish. He knows much more than you do! He has far more potential in mind for you than you could imagine (Eph. 3:20). If you insist on mapping out your own strategy, you'll miss the joy of participating in *his* plans.

Fifth, don't expect God's will to make perfect sense to you. God's thinking is far different from ours (Isa. 55:8–9). Faith involves believing God even when you don't know how everything will work out (Heb. 11:1).

Finally, when you know what God wants you to do, do it with all your heart! This is the essence of walking joyfully with him and doing his will.

Questions for Reflection

1. How did you obtain your current job? Was it the result of carefully seeking God's will? If not, could that explain some of the difficulties you may now be experiencing?
2. What method do you go through as you seek God's will? How could you improve this method?
3. Explain the difference between pursuing a God-given plan for your life and pursuing God's will, then adjusting your life to it?

Additional Resources

Deuteronomy 30:11–21
1 Samuel 2:35
John 14:16–18; 16:7–15; 17:3
Ephesians 2:10; 5:17
James 4:17

Henry Blackaby, *Created to Be God's Friend: How God Shapes Those He Loves* (Nashville: Thomas Nelson, 1999).

Henry Blackaby and Richard Blackaby, Claude King, *Experiencing God: Knowing and Doing the Will of God, Revised Edition* (Nashville: LifeWay Press, 2007).

Andrew Murray, *God's Plans for You* (Springdale, PA: Whitaker House, 1983).

How do I "wait on the Lord" when "time is money"?

Some people would rather climb Mount Everest or drain the Amazon River than wait, even on God. Waiting on the Lord is one of the most challenging exercises Christians undertake. Successful business operators and other leaders are doers, people of action. Results are their measuring stick for success. Financial ruin awaits the slow of foot. Yet problems arise when such initiative preempts God's will.

To a dynamic leader, waiting is an annoyance and makes no business sense. Time is money. Idleness is for the lazy—a luxury that industrious people cannot afford. But most Christians seem to have a profound misunderstanding of what it means to wait on the Lord.

Waiting on God is *not* inactivity. In fact, it can be the most strenuous and productive thing we do. God is far more determined to accomplish his work than we are. God does not squander time, and neither should we. However, the Bible and Christian history substantiate that God prepares his people so they are usable for his purposes. The primary message of biblical prophets was for God's people to return to him and to become holy. *Then* God would use them to bring salvation to the world's nations. If we refuse to allow him the time to orient us to his activity, how can we know what he is concerned about? Waiting on the Lord is not inactivity. It is the dynamic process of seeking his agenda.

What does waiting on the Lord look like? When you lack a clear sense of direction for what God wants you to do, that is the time to wait on him. Suppose you have been offered a new job that requires an immediate decision. But God has not given you assurance that you should accept the offer. Do you succumb to the pressure and seize the position, assuming if God did not want you to have the job, he would not have given you the opportunity? Some foolishly and unbiblically pray, "Lord, if this is not your will, please shut the door on this opportunity." Circumstances alone never provide a definitive guidance for decision making. God has the answer. Look to him for his directives.

How do you wait on the Lord? Waiting on the Lord does not mean procrastinating or charging forward, hoping for a lightning bolt. Waiting, paradoxically, is an activity. Spend time in God's presence. Pore over his Word. Schedule *unhurried time* with God. That may mean devoting some early mornings to him, spending a day alone, or getting away to a secluded place for a weekend to seek God's face. If you rush in and out of his presence, don't expect him to give you a profound revelation out of the blue. Go to God humbly and reverently, and set aside ample time to spend with him. Carefully study Scripture and allow the Holy Spirit to use its words to speak to you. Spend time praying—and don't do all the talking! Remain silent before your Creator. Allow God to open your understanding to the Scriptures as you read them (Luke 24:27, 32).

How long should you wait on the Lord? What if you miss an opportunity by not immediately seizing it? It is far more regrettable to *not* have sought God's will in a decision than to hurry up and decide without having heard from God.

Depending on the situation, you may need to linger before the Lord over several days, weeks, months, even years (Luke 2:25–28, 36–38). Of course you must continue your daily responsibilities, but you should seek to foster a steady spiritual attentiveness to God throughout the day and during your devotional times with him. Waiting on the Lord is a spiritual state wherein you heighten your sensitivity to whatever the Spirit is saying. It is living with an expectant, attentive heart. Be prepared—God may seek first to cleanse your life, mind, and heart so you can clearly hear the word he gives you in due time. Waiting on the Lord reminds you that apart from abiding in Christ, you can do nothing (John 15:5).

Questions for Reflection

1. Do you find waiting on the Lord difficult? If so, why?
2. Does God have you waiting on him right now? If so, what are you learning from him?
3. What have you been doing as you wait on the Lord? What else could you do?
4. Have you regretted not waiting on the Lord? If so, what was the result of your impatience?

Additional Resources

Deuteronomy 30:11–20
Jeremiah 29:11
Psalms 25:3; 25:21; 27:14; 33:20; 37:7; 37:9; 37:34; 40:1; 46:10; 106:13
Isaiah 40:31; 41:10, 13
John 14:15, 21, 23–24

Henry Blackaby and Richard Blackaby, Claude King, *Experiencing God: Knowing and Doing the Will of God, Revised Edition* (Nashville: LifeWay Press, 2007).

Henry Blackaby and Richard Blackaby, *Hearing God's Voice* (Nashville: Broadman & Holman, 2002).

Henry Blackaby and Richard Blackaby, *When God Speaks: How to Hear from God and Respond in Obedience* (Nashville: LifeWay Press, 1995).

What are the main purposes of prayer?

Jesus taught his disciples many wonderful things, but according to Scripture, one activity particularly intrigued them. There is no biblical record that the twelve ever asked Jesus to teach them how to preach or heal the sick or walk on water. They did ask him, however, to teach them to pray (Luke 11:1). In response, Jesus gave them a model prayer, an outline for how to pray (Matt. 6:9–13; Luke 11:2–4). The Lord's Prayer provides a compelling model for us, as well.

Here are six characteristics of God-honoring prayer:

1. *Prayer begins in submission to God's will.* If we do not approach God with a willingness to obey whatever he says, there is no point in praying. In a poignant moment, Jesus cried out, "My Father! If it is possible, let this cup pass from Me. Yet not as I will, but as You will" (Matt. 26:39). Jesus honestly shared his human preference, but he simultaneously submitted to his Father's sovereignty. Likewise, our prayers must focus on aligning our will to the Father's, not pleading with God to fulfill our dreams.

2. *Genuine prayer is rooted in faith.* Prayer, by its nature, implies we trust God to hear us and to respond. Failure to pray signifies a lack of belief in prayer's power and efficacy. Difficulty in finding time to pray is not a time-management problem. It reflects our doubt that prayer really makes a difference in our life or in the world around us. Those who truly believe

that God answers prayer will spend time praying. It is impossible to please God without faith (Heb. 11:6). Jesus said: "Therefore, I tell you, all the things you pray and ask for—believe that you have received them, and you will have them" (Mark 11:24). If our prayers are not being answered, that is not an indictment on prayer in general but on the way we are praying.

3. *Prayer requires perseverance.* Tenacity in praying demonstrates our desperation for God to intervene on our behalf. Should God respond to lackadaisical, distracted prayers? As Jesus walked along the road outside Jericho, a crowd swarmed him. Sitting by the roadside was Bartimaeus, a blind man (Mark 10:46–52). Bartimaeus couldn't know exactly when Jesus would pass by, so he kept crying out, "Jesus, Son of David, have mercy on me!" Jesus' disciples urged Bartimaeus to be silent; Jesus was surrounded by people, and he needed to travel on to Jerusalem. Yet Bartimaeus knew that Jesus was his only hope. *Nothing* would deter him from gaining Jesus' attention. So he persisted. And Jesus heard his urgent voice. After healing Bartimaeus, Jesus explained, "Your faith has healed you" (Mark 10:52). Bartimaeus's determination proved his faith, and for that he was bountifully rewarded.

4. *God-honoring prayer requires that we pursue him with all our heart, mind, soul, and strength* (Matt. 7:7–11; Mark 12:30). God promised we will find him when we seek him wholeheartedly (Jer. 29:12–13). When we draw near to God, he *will* draw near to us (James 4:8). Prayer is not merely reciting our requests or muttering pious phrases. It is drawing near to God. Why is prayer so important to the believer? The world is constantly luring believers *away* from God. Prayer is the God-ordained vehicle that drives us back to him. Prolonged neglect of prayer has a debilitating effect on a Christian's soul. The longer we forsake prayer, the farther we inevitably drift from God.

5. *Prayer is a divine encounter.* God-honoring prayer must be wrapped in holiness. The prophet Isaiah entered holy God's magnificent presence and was immediately overwhelmed by his own sinfulness (Isa. 6:5). God

warned that he would not hear the prayers of those who were practicing sin (Isa. 1:15; 59:1–2). Ironically, many unbelievers reject God because they claim to have prayed for something and God did not do what they asked. Such people must understand that God listens to only one prayer by unbelievers, and that is their prayer of repentance for their sin (Isa. 59:1–3, 12). Similarly, Christians who think they can live as they please, carelessly disregarding God's commandments and refusing to obey his will, and yet expect God to heed all their prayers are misguided. It is a sacred experience to enter into Almighty God's presence, coming face-to-face with our holy Creator.

6. *We are invited to enter into God's presence with boldness* (Heb. 10:19). Complementing the reality of God's holiness is the wonderful truth that, although we are sinners, God has adopted us into his royal family so we can cry out to God as our dear Father (Rom. 8:14–17). Just as children of earthly monarchs have access to the throne room unimagined by commoners, our Father *wants* us to enter the most sacred place in the universe, his presence, not cavalierly but confidently.

Prayer is not an exercise where we drone on to God, reciting our litany of needs and desires, laying out everything we want God to do for us and for others. God already knows what we require far better than we do. He actually wants to do exceedingly more than we have in mind (Eph. 3:20). If our prayer time is a daily litany of the same entreaties, we will miss his agenda. But if we take time to listen, God has amazing things he wants to accomplish in and through our lives (Jer. 29:11–14).

He is God! His ways are not our ways (Isa. 55:8–9). His thinking transcends ours. We can't imagine what we should be praying and asking him to do. The only way for us to know God's heart is for him to reveal it to us. God wants us to care about the same things that concern him (1 Sam. 2:35). Prayer is the opportunity to join our heart with his. How incredible that Almighty God wants to share intimately with us! How bewildering that God's people would be too busy to let him do so! Those who find themselves too distracted and self-centered to listen to God grossly exaggerate the importance of their activity and woefully underestimate the wonder of hearing from God.

Questions for Reflection

1. Evaluate your prayer life. How does it line up with the six characteristics listed in this chapter?
2. Do you find praying difficult? If so, why?
3. Do you think God is pleased with the way you pray? What adjustments to your prayer life would honor him?
4. What has God said to you in prayer lately? Are you giving God sufficient time to speak to you? If not, what specific changes should you make in your prayer times?

Additional Resources

Isaiah 6:1–6; 58:16
Jeremiah 7:13
Ezekiel 22:30–31
Mark 1:35–38
Luke 5:16, 6:12, 9:28–32, 11:1–4; 18:1–8, 22:39–46
John 17

Henry Blackaby and Norman Blackaby, *Experiencing Prayer with Jesus: The Power of His Presence and Example* (Sisters, OR: Multnomah, 2006).
E. M. Bounds, *The Necessity of Prayer* (Springdale, PA: Whitaker House, 1984).
E. M. Bounds, *Power through Prayer* (Grand Rapids, MI: Baker Book House, 1972).

E. M. Bounds, *Prayer and Praying Men* (Grand Rapids, MI: Baker Book House, 1991).

Dick Eastman, *No Easy Road: Inspirational Thoughts on Prayer* (Grand Rapids, MI: Baker Book House, 1971).

S. D. Gordon, *Quiet Talks on Prayer* (New York: Fleming H. Revell, 1904).

O. Hallesby, *Prayer* (Minneapolis: Augsburg Publishing House, 1931).

T. W. Hunt, *The Doctrine of Prayer* (Nashville: Convention Press, 1986).

D. L. Moody, *Prevailing Prayer* (Chicago: Moody Press, n.d.).

Andrew Murray, *With Christ in the School of Prayer* (Springdale, PA: Whitaker House, 1981).

George S. Stewart, *The Lower Levels of Prayer* (New York: Abingdon Press, 1940).

How do I meditate on God's Word?

Christians in the Western world can be uncomfortable with meditation, associating the practice with Eastern mysticism. But meditation is a biblical practice that can lead to life-changing encounters with God. Through meditation we can go deeper with God and gain profound insights from him.

Meditation can occupy a brief period or an extended time span. At times, circumstances may compel us to quickly focus on God's Word. Psalm 46:1 says that God is a "helper who is always found in times of trouble." In moments of need, we can experience the reality of God's presence immediately. Likewise, through the psalmist, God instructs us to be still "and know that I am God" (Ps. 46:10). In the calm, quiet moments of our lives, or in the middle of a hectic day, we can become keenly aware that God is with us. We can pause at any hour to contemplate what God has promised us through his Word.

It is also wise to devote extended periods of time to hearing from God. Jesus often made time in his schedule for prolonged prayer sessions with his Father. He would go to a mountain to pray throughout the night (Mark 6:46; Luke 6:12). He would rise early to enable solitary, uninterrupted communion with his Father (Mark 1:35). These encounters were Jesus' lifeline as he constantly sought to align himself with his Father's will.

To clearly hear from God on weighty issues, it is not prudent to launch a hurried prayer on the way to the boardroom or staff meeting. Some matters are so vital, they demand that we do whatever is necessary to hear from God. This may require sacrifice on our part, as Jesus demonstrated, but obtaining God's divine wisdom is well worth going without sleep or food.

Meditation sometimes involves sustained concentration, focusing on God for several days, weeks, or even months. Twice, Moses spent forty days and nights on Mount Sinai receiving God's message (Deut. 9:9, 25). Jesus, too, spent forty days and nights in the wilderness as he prepared to commence his public ministry (Matt. 4:1–2; Luke 4:1–2). The apostle Paul spent three years in Arabia allowing God to prepare his heart and mind for God's great work through his life (Gal. 1:15–18).

Even if you cannot retreat to be alone, you can maintain an elevated level of spiritual concentration and watchfulness. A time of extended focus on God is crucial when you are facing a major decision or undergoing difficult circumstances. At such times, you need God to walk particularly closely with you. Throughout the days and weeks, God may use a variety of means to communicate his heart. He will build upon what he said earlier until, over time, you gain a full understanding of what he is teaching you.

Here are several truths to consider regarding meditation:

1. *To meditate is to remain in God's presence until you clearly hear from him.* Christians rush in and out of God's presence, yet they expect to gain understanding of profound, divine realities. Meditation is a discipline wherein you focus long enough for God to lead you into a deep encounter with him (2 Cor. 3:18), allowing the time for God to teach you scriptural truths at a deeper level than usual. Eastern mysticism uses meditation to empty the mind; biblical meditation is focused concentration on what God says about a specific subject. It helps you comprehend the magnitude of Christ's suffering on the cross or more fully grasp the multifaceted reality of God's character. Meditation leads to a deeper understanding of God's truth—the truth that sets you free (John 8:32).

2. Some religions encourage you to repeat the same phrases over and over while you meditate. Biblical meditation is not a practice of speaking but of hearing from God. The Spirit of truth is prepared to guide you, but you must remain silent before him and listen to him (John 16:13).

3. Meditation is God-centered, not self-centered. The primary focus of meditation is to know God more fully and intimately (Jer. 9:23–24). Christ can present himself so simply that a child can enjoy a sweet relationship with him. He can also offer glimpses of his character that are so phenomenal, they baffle the sharpest human mind. When you meditate, you take time to concentrate on God so he reveals new insights into his nature. Regardless of how much time you spend in this pursuit, there will always be more to learn because God is infinite.

4. The secondary purpose of meditation is to better understand ourselves and our circumstances. Pondering our spiritual condition can prevent sin from gaining a foothold in our heart. The automatic by-product of an encounter with God is seeing ourselves as we are (Job 42:1–6; Isa. 6:5). The downfall of many leaders occurs because they don't take time to understand their own weaknesses and God's corresponding strength.

5. Meditation can be enhanced through fasting. Fasting takes the emphasis off your physical appetites so you can satisfy your spiritual need. Every distraction that can be removed while you meditate will channel your concentration and receptivity to hear more clearly from God.

Meditation can enable you to experience profound insights into God's Word. It can forever change your life. Set aside time for meditation so you can begin to go deeper with God.

Questions for Reflection

1. How often do you meditate on the Lord and his Word?
2. What are some issues that call for extra wisdom wherein you could benefit from meditation?

3. What truths or Scriptures do you feel would greatly enrich you if you were to meditate on them?
4. What steps can you take to facilitate meditation?

Additional Resources

Psalms 1:1–6; 24:3–6; 46:10; 119:15; 119:27; 119:97; 119:148
Proverbs 3:5–8
Jeremiah 9:23–24
Luke 2:40, 52
James 4:8

T. W. Hunt, *The Mind of Christ: The Transforming Power of Thinking His Thoughts* (Nashville: Broadman & Holman, 1995).
Andrew Murray, *Like Christ* (Springdale, PA: Whitaker House, 1981).

How can I pray for the people at work?

Intercessory prayer is characterized by its *intensity* and *focus*. People are sometimes in particularly urgent need of God's intervention. For some, God's judgment is imminent unless they turn from their sin. Others face circumstances that threaten to overwhelm them. Whether it's a serious illness, a financial crisis, or a major personal decision, you have the privilege of petitioning the Lord on others' behalf.

Intercessory prayer is recorded throughout the Scriptures. When the Hebrew people sinned grievously, God prepared to utterly destroy them until Moses pleaded with God on their behalf. The Israelites were oblivious to their imminent peril, but Moses was not. He offered up this remarkably selfless intercession for them: "Oh, this people has committed a great sin; they have made for themselves a god of gold. Now if You would only forgive their sin. But if not, please erase me from the book You have written" (Exod. 32:31–32). Incredibly, Moses was willing to sacrifice his own eternity to spare his sinful countrymen.

Likewise, the government leader Daniel voiced a tremendous prayer for his people (Dan. 9:3–19). He concluded with this plea:

> Therefore, our God, hear the prayer and the petitions of
> Your servant. Show Your favor to Your desolate sanctuary for

the Lord's sake. Listen, my God, and hear. Open Your eyes and see our desolations and the city called by Your name. For we are not presenting our petitions before You based on our righteous acts, but based on Your abundant compassion. Lord, hear! Lord, forgive! Lord, listen and act! My God, for Your own sake, do not delay, because Your city and Your people are called by Your name. (Dan. 9:17–19)

Daniel, the most righteous person of his era, wholly identified with the sins of his people and pled with God for forgiveness.

It is one thing to have influence with people. It is quite another to have influence with God. The Bible indicates that some men and women had such a quality walk with God that he readily responded to their prayers. God identified Moses and Samuel as intercessors holding high standing with him (Jer. 15:1). Daniel was so esteemed in heaven that an angel was dispatched to him the moment he began praying (Dan. 9:23). Hannah prayed so fervently that God heeded her desperate plea (1 Sam. 1:10–17). Christ continually makes intercession for the saints (Heb. 7:25).

The Bible records a tragic lack of intercessors in Old Testament times: "'I searched for a man among them who would repair the wall and stand in the gap before Me on behalf of the land so that I might not destroy it, but I found no one. So I have poured out My indignation on them and consumed them with the fire of My fury. I have brought their actions down on their own heads.' This is the declaration of the Lord GOD" (Ezek. 22:30–31).

What about our generation? Do we understand the power of intercessory prayer? We must learn to be spiritual advocates for others. The following four aspects of intercessory prayer apply to you in your workplace:

First, as a Christian you are automatically a spiritual liaison for your colleagues. God expects you to participate in his activity in your midst. God may have specifically placed you in your present position so that he has a Christian who can stand in the gap for your coworkers.

Second, consider the circle of contacts your job gives you. There are needs all around you, and people whom you could be representing in prayer before God. Ask God to open your understanding so you see what he sees (Mark 8:17–18). Amid the frenzied rush of activity and interchange of secular business, God can sensitize you to hurting people around you, people who urgently need hope from the Lord. A colleague may be under enormous job pressures. Perhaps an employee is entangled in a painful divorce. Another may be held hostage by an addiction. Your associate could be stricken with disease or enduring the loneliness of recent widowhood. You would be astonished to learn what plagues the men and women with whom you do business every day.

Third, while you can't possibly be aware of every person's situation, you can ask God to guide you in your prayers. Take time to pray compassionately for those people God lays on your heart. God wants to do a work in their lives, and he is looking for someone to mediate for them. God's Word instructs us to pray for those in need (James 5:13–18). As we pray for people, we will better understand God's heart for them. In addition, we will experience the joy of seeing God work in their lives.

Finally, be prepared to pay a price. Intercession can be a sacrificial enterprise; it takes time and energy, and it may take a toll on your emotions. When Hannah beseeched the Lord for a son, she vowed that she would give him to God. God answered her, and she kept her promise though it cost the joy of rearing her own child.

We know a Christian executive who faithfully prayed for his company and let people know he was interceding for them. His CEO became so antagonistic about this that he eventually forced the Christian out of the company. Yet God vindicated his faithful servant. Before long that same CEO was asking his former employee to pray for him in a personal need he was facing. As you pray for others, understand that God may use *you* to answer your own prayers. Be willing to reach out as God leads and to give of your time or resources as the Lord directs you.

The influence of an intercessor in the marketplace is immeasurable. There is no limit to what God can do through those willing to stand in the gap for their companies and the people with whom they interact.

Questions for Reflection

1. Do you intercede for the people with whom you do business? If not, why not?
2. How could you be a more effective intercessor for your company?
3. Has God opened your eyes to the needs of your colleagues and employees? In what ways can you intercede for these? Has he asked you to make a personal sacrifice to help those for whom you are praying? If so, what are you going to do?

Additional Resources

2 Chronicles 16:9
Ezra 9:5–8
Luke 22:31–32
John 17
Romans 9:1–5
Ephesians 1:15–23
Philippians 1:3–4

E. M. Bounds, *Prayer and Praying Men* (Grand Rapids, MI: Baker Book House, 1991).

Oswald Chambers, *If You Will Ask* (n.p.: Discovery House Publishers, 1989).

Norman Grubb, *Rees Howell: Intercessor* (n.p.: Christian Literature Crusade, 1998).

Rob Finley, *Recapturing Biblical Intercession* (Memphis: Prayer Resources, n.d.).

Gregory R. Frizzell, *How to Develop a Powerful Prayer Life* (Memphis: The Master Design, 1999).

Andrew Murray, *The Ministry of Intercessory Prayer* (Minneapolis: Bethany House, 2003).

Oswald Sanders, *Prayer Power Unlimited* (Chicago: Moody Press, 1997).

How can I get the most out of studying God's Word and clearly understand what God is telling me?

We know businesspeople who read and assimilate complex technical books on engineering or computer science. Others can scan reams of labyrinthine financial reports and immediately spot an error. Yet these same people are intimidated by the Bible sitting in front of them. They are bewildered, not knowing where to begin in their Bible study.

When these men and women come to a crisis, they know they need to hear from God. So they open their Bibles but are unsure of what to read. Many verses don't seem applicable to them. They are unsure if their predicament is even addressed in the Scriptures. But God said his Word is not merely *important* to our life; it *is* our life (Deut. 32:46–47). Knowing how to study God's Word is imperative so we can gain his perspective on our situation.

Here are some guidelines to enrich your devotional studies:

1. Settle in your heart and mind that you are reading God's Holy Word. The Bible has no equal in literature. There is no other means through which God speaks as clearly and forcefully as through Scripture.

Open your Bible with a readiness to obey whatever God says (Jer. 9:23–24; John 14:21, 23). If you approach your Bible as a skeptic, you may seek a word from God in vain.

2. *Recognize who is speaking to you through the pages of Scripture.* God's Spirit of truth will open your understanding to the words you read (John 14:26; 16:13–15). You do not dig up truth. Truth is revealed by the Holy Spirit. Therefore, you may read a passage you have seen many times, but suddenly the words speak powerfully to you as never before. As the Spirit addresses your current situation, he opens up specific verses to your deeper understanding. Be careful not to stifle the Holy Spirit's activity in your life by resisting his directives, for you do not want to miss what God has to say to you (1 Cor. 2:9–12).

3. *Be purposeful in your Bible study.* The best way to walk through God's Word is to be consistent. Don't neglect your Bible and then, when a crisis hits, randomly leaf through its pages hoping to glean a helpful verse. Rather, daily immerse yourself in Scripture so you have the full counsel of the Bible to guide you. While not ruling out the spontaneity of God's directing you to a particular book, we recommend that you read from several parts of the Bible each day. We like to study a chapter of Proverbs every day (there is one chapter for each day of the month). Also, reading a chapter from the Gospels daily will enable you to read through the four Gospels each year. This keeps the model of Jesus' life always before you. You could also read an additional chapter from both the Old and New Testaments. Or you might choose to read right through a particular book, like Deuteronomy or Romans. Second Timothy 3:16 proclaims, "All Scripture is inspired by God, and is profitable." Regularly submit your life to every part of Scripture so you lack nothing from the wisdom God shares through his Word.

4. *Keep a journal.* Take careful notes when you read God's Word. *God* is speaking, and anything he says is worth writing down for remembering and reviewing (Mal. 3:16–18; Rev. 1:1–3, 19).

A devotional journal is a great resource for recounting God's activity in your life. For instance, let's say your company asks you to transfer to the corporate office in Asia. Initially, you may be shocked as you have never considered an international posting, and you are terribly concerned about uprooting your family. As you survey your journal, however, you recall how powerfully God spoke to you through Genesis as you read how Abraham left all he knew to go to a land God would show him. You even wrote in your journal how tragic it would have been if Abraham had missed this opportunity to follow God to the promised land. Your journal may also remind you how stirred you were by the Great Commission (Matt. 28:18–20). You wrote, "What am I and my family doing to impact the world with the gospel?" Reading back through your journal may help you see that God has actually been working in your life for months, preparing you for an international assignment. Through God's Word, the Spirit of truth has been preparing you for what he knew was in your future. It is important to keep track of everything God says to you through his Word, because doing so will prove invaluable to you when you are seeking his guidance in the future.

5. *Use Scripture to confirm Scripture.* When you sense God has spoken to you through his Word, verify the message with other passages. It is dangerous to rush off in a life direction based on one verse. It is possible to misinterpret Scripture, so the safest approach is to ensure that what you conclude from one verse is borne out in other passages. It is also vital to understand the nature of various portions of Scripture. (A good Bible dictionary or study Bible can help with this.) For example, poetic literature is not meant to be taken literally. Likewise, the epistles were written to apply universal truths to a particular place and time. Also bear in mind that the Bible honestly records what people did, but it is not necessarily advocating that we do the same!

6. *Verify what you believe God's Word is telling you.* While you should always go straight to Scripture to receive a word from God, you can confirm

his message by talking with others and seeking their perspective. If you sense God's speaking to you through a Scripture passage, share it with your prayer partner or Bible study group. Spiritually perceptive friends will recognize a word from God. Make use, too, of reputable biblical commentaries to ensure that what you're finding in the Bible is confirmed by those who have studied God's Word in depth.

We all know sincere Christians who stumbled upon a verse, then accepted an out-of-context interpretation that was contrary to the true meaning of the text. As a result, they made an ill-advised life decision. They met with predictable disaster. It is critical to ask the Holy Spirit to affirm through other believers what you sense he is saying to you. A word of caution is in order here. Once you have clearly heard from God, it can be an act of disobedience to keep hashing it over with others and asking for signs rather than obeying what God has said. Fellow believers can help you clarify what God has said, but the time will come for your obedient response.

7. *Surround yourself with God's Word so it permeates your thoughts and shapes your attitudes.* Keep pertinent passages before you, posted at your desk, in your vehicle, or in your hotel room as you travel. Discipline yourself to memorize Scripture, and the Holy Spirit will bring verses to mind at crucial moments (Ps. 119:11, 15–16).

8. *Keep God's Word in mind at all times* (Ps. 1:2–3; 4:4; 77:6; 119:15, 27, 97, 148). The Bible is so profound, it demands careful contemplation so you can understand the full richness contained in its pages. The Scriptures are dynamic and multifaceted; one verse can have many applications and depths of meaning. Meditation helps reveal dimensions of Scripture you would otherwise miss.

God's Word overflows with rich, life-changing truths. Make every effort to mine its treasures and to hear what God has to say to you.

Questions for Reflection

1. How much time do you spend seriously probing God's Word? Could you extend that time?
2. What are some ways you might enrich the time you spend studying God's Word?
3. Are there sections of the Bible you do not know well? Develop a plan to study them in the next year.
4. What resources (commentaries, study Bibles, Bible CDs, Bible dictionaries, Bible atlas) would help you be a better student of God's Word? Plan to acquire them and use them.

Additional Resources

Psalms 1:1–6; 78:1–8; 119
Luke 24:27
Ephesians 3:14–21
Hebrews 2:1–4, 4:12–13; 12:25–26

Henry Blackaby, Richard Blackaby, Thomas Blackaby, Melvin Blackaby, and Norman Blackaby, *The Blackaby Study Bible* (Nashville: Thomas Nelson, 2006).

Henry Blackaby and Richard Blackaby, *Hearing God's Voice,* (Nashville: Broadman & Holman, 2002).

Henry Blackaby, Melvin Blackaby, and Norman Blackaby, *Encounters with God: Transforming Your Bible Study* (Nashville: Thomas Nelson, 2007).

Robertson McQuilkin, *Understanding and Applying the Bible* (Chicago: Moody Press, 1983; revised ed., 1992).

How do I know when I'm hearing from God?

There is no more important issue for Christians than recognizing when God is speaking. Failing to identify God's voice brings devastating consequences. Jesus said, "My sheep hear My voice, I know them, and they follow Me" (John 10:27). Some who are uncomfortable with the truth that God speaks to people have suggested this verse refers only to salvation. But the obvious truth, as borne out in Scripture and throughout church history, is that if you are one of Jesus' sheep, you *will* know the voice of your Shepherd (John 10:2–5).

One day Jesus' disciples asked him why he explained his teachings to them more fully than he did to the crowds:

> The disciples came up and asked Him, "Why do You speak to them in parables?"
>
> He answered them, "Because the secrets of the kingdom of heaven have been given for you to know, but it has not been given to them. For whoever has more will be given to him, and he will have more than enough. But whoever does not have, even what he has will be taken away from him. For this reason I speak to them in parables, because looking they do not see, and hearing they do not listen or understand. Isaiah's

prophecy is fulfilled in them, which says: "You will listen and listen, yet never understand; and you will look and look, and never perceive. For this people's heart has grown callous; their ears are hard of hearing, and they have shut their eyes; otherwise they might see with their eyes and hear with their ears, understand with their hearts and turn back—and I would cure them." But your eyes are blessed because they do see, and your ears because they do hear! For I assure you: Many prophets and righteous people longed to see the things you see yet didn't see them; to hear the things you hear yet didn't hear them. (Matt. 13:10–17)

When Jesus preached to the multitudes, he often taught with parables. He spoke much more plainly to his twelve disciples. His Father had given the disciples to him, and Jesus knew he was to teach them everything his Father gave to him (John 16:14–15; 17:8). Jesus ensured that his followers received every truth his Father wanted him to communicate. Likewise, he will give you the opportunity to hear every truth the heavenly Father wishes to dispense to you. The question is whether you will recognize his voice when he does.

Jesus does not speak the same way to everyone. He will communicate with his people, however, in ways we understand. As we walk with the Lord and listen attentively, we will learn to recognize the various ways he speaks to us. But if we immerse ourselves in the din of the world and neglect to spend time in prayer and meditation, we will not develop a familiarity with God's voice. It is not that God does not speak but that we become disoriented to him and do not hear him.

People have asked: "How can I know if what I'm hearing comes from God or from Satan?" Anyone who can't tell the difference between God's voice and Satan's lies is in great peril! There are several ways you can ensure that what you are hearing is from God. Some of them have been mentioned in earlier answers regarding studying God's Word, so we will briefly summarize them below.

First, regularly spend time communing with God so you become attuned to his voice. God is a Person. He will relate to you individually and personally. The more time you spend with him, the more easily you will distinguish his voice (John 14:9).

Second, study the Gospels to see how Jesus spoke to people. Notice his compassion toward those who were hurting. Observe his response to the proud and self-righteous. Pay attention to his words to sinners. God does not change (Mal. 3:6). The more you immerse yourself in Jesus' life and the way he communicates, the more readily you will recognize when he is speaking to you.

Third, prepare yourself to hear from God. God warns, "If your heart turns away and you do not listen . . ." (Deut. 30:17). You must soften your heart so when God's Word comes, you are receptive to it (Matt. 13:1–9). If you have become hardened to spiritual things, you won't hear God speak.

Fourth, verify with Scripture what you are hearing (Acts 17:11). God will never contradict his written Word. For example, God will never suspend his hatred of sin for your special circumstances. He will not cease to be true to his nature in the way he deals with you. People have told us God released them from any obligation to seek reconciliation with an estranged fellow Christian. We wondered, "When did God rescind his command to be reconciled?" (Matt. 5:23–24). Couples have claimed God sanctioned their adulterous relationship because of their love for each other. But God would have to ignore His own word and nature to do so (Exod. 20:14; Prov. 5; 6:20–35; Matt. 5:27–32; Mark 10:1–12). The more familiar you are with God's Word, the easier it will be to recognize when God is speaking and when he is not.

Fifth, allow the Holy Spirit to confirm in your spirit that what you are hearing is from God. Just as the Spirit verifies you are God's child (Rom. 8:16), so the Spirit will validate a message from God. If your soul is troubled, perhaps what you are hearing is not from God. We have known people who felt deeply uneasy about a crucial decision, but they proceeded anyway. The results were catastrophic. They cried out to God, "How could you let this happen?" In fact, they had continued in their disastrous direction despite the Spirit's warning.

Sixth, seek verification from fellow believers that what you have heard is from God. When a dispute arose in the early church regarding religious practices, the church leaders sought God's leadership together, and they clearly found God's will on the subject (Acts 15:1–41).

Seventh, trust that God always carries through on his Word (Isa. 46:10–11; 55:10–11; Matt. 5:18). If God is behind a decision, the proof will be the outcome. In the Old Testament, the substantiation that God had spoken to a prophet was that what the prophet proclaimed actually occurred (Deut. 18:21–22). Some people are continually claiming to receive a word from the Lord, yet time reveals that none of their alleged revelations come to pass. Moreover, the claimants readily abandon their previous revelation when a new one comes along. Conversely, God finishes what he starts. If you sense God may be leading you to take action, watch carefully to see if God is affirming your decision in practical, tangible ways. And check to see that the "fresh word" does not contradict the last thing he told you.

Finally, test whether you are hearing from God by considering what the result of following that word would be. God's words are "a lamp for my feet and a light on my path" (Ps. 119:105). Following his guidance will always lead you closer to him, and this will inevitably bring joy (Luke 10:17; John 15:11). Likewise, God will not lead you to an action that will destroy your family or harm your church. If every time you act on what you think is a word from God the result is failure and heartache, it probably is not a divine word you are following.

Hearing from God and recognizing his voice are foundational to the Christian life. If you pay close attention and respond in obedience, you will experience God in ways you never thought possible.

Questions for Reflection

1. How have you prepared your life to receive a word from God?
2. What have you heard God saying over the last few weeks?
3. How have you verified that what you heard is from God?
4. How can you better equip yourself to hear from God?

Additional Resources

Deuteronomy 15:5; 30:17
Joshua 1:7–9
Isaiah 55:10–11
Matthew 4:4
John 14:23–24; 15:15; 16:12–15

Henry Blackaby and Richard Blackaby, Claude King, *Experiencing God: Knowing and Doing the Will of God, Revised Edition* (Nashville: LifeWay Press, 2007).

Henry Blackaby and Richard Blackaby, *Hearing God's Voice* (Nashville: Broadman & Holman, 2002).

Henry Blackaby and Richard Blackaby, *When God Speaks: How to Recognize God's Voice and Respond in Obedience* (Nashville: LifeWay Press, 1986).

What do I do when God seems silent?

God's word is our life: "Man does not live on bread alone but on every word that comes from the mouth of the LORD" (Deut. 8:3). It is crucial to always know when God is speaking. However, people do experience periods of silence, when periods of time can pass without divine direction or guidance. This is always difficult, but it is especially so when an important decision looms.

When such times come, there are several things you can do:

1. Diligently ensure that sin has not dulled your spiritual sensitivity. When your heart is turned away from God, you will not hear from Him (Deut. 30:17). The first place to look when you are not hearing from God is to your own heart. Sin deafens us spiritually. God could be speaking mightily to those all around you, yet you might not recognize his voice. Turn your heart over to God and ask him to reveal any sin so you can deal with it (Ps. 139:23–24).

2. Nurture a close relationship with God so you know how to recognize his voice. Simply going through the motions of the Christian life without spending extended time in his Word and in prayer will not help you when you desperately need a word from God. The best way to recognize when God is speaking is to spend lots of time with him, building an intimate bond. Then you will recognize his voice when you hear it (John 10:27).

3. *Make certain you take time to really listen.* As a business leader, you may be accustomed to power lunches and fifteen minute conference calls. Be careful, however, that you do not seek to squeeze Almighty God into your schedule in fifteen minute increments. He is God. He deserves your best. He deserves your rapt attention. Strive for unhurried time with God. Schedule enough time with him that you do not feel compelled to fidget and to keep looking at your watch. Allow plenty of time to lay your heart before God and, more importantly, to hear all God has to say to you. He does not hand out profound truths like burgers at a drive-through window. God will speak to us on his terms, not ours.

4. *Turn off the TV.* Ignore the phone. Set aside the laptop and whatever electronic device is commanding your attention—not forever, but for a time. If you shut out the cacophony of worldly noise, it might surprise you how much easier it is to hear from God. Why should God compete for your attention? He is God! Today's electronic wizardry allows us instant access to almost anything, and the services they provide can become addictive. These devices may be impediments to hearing from God.

5. *Consider your spiritual accountability.* Have you obeyed the previous word God gave you? Why would he give you step two if you neglected to take step one? We can't pick and choose which divine directives we will obey, leapfrogging over whatever does not appeal to us. Each spiritual step of growth builds on the last one. To receive a fresh word from God, be certain you followed up on the last thing he told you.

6. *Understand that you may not yet be ready for God's word.* Jesus told his disciples, "I still have many things to tell you, but you can't bear them now" (John 16:12). Christ knew what lay ahead for each disciple. He understood the oppression they would endure. He was aware of the Father's plans for all twelve men. But he knew they were not ready yet. They needed time to process what he had already taught them, to adjust their lives to those truths and to grow in their faith. They did not yet possess the spiritual maturity to receive all Christ had to share with them. If you

are not hearing a new word from God, use the time to grow as a Christian and in your understanding of spiritual things. Just as the Holy Spirit would in time teach the disciples all things (John 16:13–15), be patient and expect him to do the same with you.

7. *Examine your prayer life.* Are you asking for things that are beneath what God wants to do in your life? (Eph. 3:20). You may be praying about superficial issues while God is patiently waiting for you to elevate your desires, praying for things to which he is pleased to respond (John 11:40). You may, for example, be concentrating on getting the most value out of your television advertising budget while God may be leading you to redirect your advertising away from TV programs that dishonor him.

If you are experiencing a period of silence with no word from God, don't despair. Consider the issues listed above and allow God to reveal the purpose for this time of silence. You may be on the brink of a fresh, divine encounter.

Questions for Reflection

1. What sins in your life could be keeping you from hearing God's voice?
2. What was the last thing God clearly told you? Were you thoroughly obedient?
3. Are you regularly spending unhurried time with God? If not, how should you adjust your schedule?
4. What noises and distractions keep you from hearing God's voice? What should you do about them?

Additional Resources

Psalms 37:7; 40:1; 46:10
Isaiah 1:15; 59:1–2; 66:4–5

Jeremiah 14:11–12; 15:1; 16:12
Habakkuk 1:1–5
John 11:1–15

Henry Blackaby and Richard Blackaby, Claude King, *Experiencing God: Knowing and Doing the Will of God, Revised Edition* (Nashville: LifeWay Press, 2007).

Henry Blackaby and Richard Blackaby, *Hearing God's Voice* (Nashville: Broadman & Holman, 2002).

Henry Blackaby and Richard Blackaby, *When God Speaks: How to Recognize God's Voice and Respond in Obedience* (Nashville: LifeWay Press, 1986).

What does it mean to "walk in the Spirit"?

There are only two ways to live: in the flesh or in the Spirit. Because of sin, we all inherit a carnal, self-centered nature. We automatically gravitate toward sin and away from God. Apart from God's saving work in our lives, we have no way to escape the spiritual bondage of the flesh. The apostle Paul said: "For the flesh desires what is against the Spirit, and the Spirit desires what is against the flesh; these are opposed to each other, so that you don't do what you want. . . . Now the works of the flesh are obvious: sexual immorality, moral impurity, promiscuity, idolatry, sorcery, hatreds, strife, jealousy, outbursts of anger, selfish ambitions, dissensions, factions, envy, drunkenness, carousing . . ." (Gal. 5:17, 19–21).

"For those whose lives are according to the flesh think about the things of the flesh, but those whose lives are according to the Spirit, about the things of the Spirit. For the mind-set of the flesh is death, but the mind-set of the Spirit is life and peace. For the mind-set of the flesh is hostile to God because if does not submit itself to God's law, for it is unable to do so. Those whose lives are in the flesh are unable to please God" (Rom. 8:5–8).

To live in the flesh is to succumb to our selfish desires, to reject God, and to embrace sin. To be in the flesh is to think like the unbelieving world and to share the same values. While our conversion transforms our corrupt spirit into a new creation, our sinful bodies are not recreated until we are resurrected from death (1 Cor. 15:42–58). We must diligently seek godliness because the world constantly appeals to our carnal appetites (Rom. 12:1–2; 1 Cor. 6:12–20; 9:27). Only by surrendering ourselves to the Spirit's control can we resist the temptations that assault us.

To live in the Spirit is to submit our lives daily to the Holy Spirit's control. When the Spirit enters our lives, he crucifies our self-centered, sinful nature. The new nature he gives us is God-centered. The evidence of the Spirit's work in our lives will be "love, joy, peace, patience, kindness, goodness, faith, gentleness, self-control" (Gal. 5:22–23). It becomes obvious who rules your spirit by examining your behavior. When people disagree with you or do not meet your expectations, if you lash out in anger, you are walking in the flesh. If you grow incensed when your achievements go unrecognized or if jealousy consumes you when someone else is succeeding, you are walking in the flesh. If someone mistreats you, yet you humbly seek reconciliation, you are walking in the Spirit. Your response to life's circumstances reveals the ruling force in your life.

Our natural default is to be guided by our flesh. If we make no effort to live for Christ, we will simply continue to live in the flesh as we always have before. Living in the Spirit requires a daily, hourly choice. It involves surrendering our will to the Holy Spirit (2 Cor. 5:17).

The problem for believers is that the world in which we live operates 100 percent in the flesh. The world in which businesspeople live and work is immersed in and obsessed with sin. We don't even have to leave the house for opportunities to dishonor God, so we must continually be on guard as every form of media delivers enticement directly to our homes. We can give in to greed, lust, infidelity, or hatred with the click of a mouse or remote control.

Our world normalizes sin to such a degree that unregenerate people all around us see nothing wrong with our carnal culture. So if we do not beseech the Spirit to control our decisions and attentions, we will be drawn quite naturally into bondage of the flesh. The apostle Paul bemoaned the fact that although he desired in his spirit to please God, his sinful flesh was constantly attracted to sin (Rom. 7:24–25).

If you are born again, you will have a deep desire in your spirit to honor and obey God. But unless you are intentional about seeking the Holy Spirit's guidance and protection from sin, you will find that the world is in you just as surely as you are in the world (John 17:11, 14–16). Take an inventory of your life at this point. Is your life radically different from that of an unbeliever? Do you *know* what God values? Do your responses to people and to temptations prove you are a child of God? Or do you blithely give the world your allegiance without discernment?

It is imperative that Christians submit to the Spirit's control. Only God can give victory over sinful flesh. We cannot afford to be apathetic about the power of evil. No matter how commonplace sin becomes in our culture, it is still as deadly as it was in the garden of Eden.

Questions for Reflection

1. Reflect on your spontaneous reactions to temptation or crises. What do they reveal about who or what is controlling your life?
2. What areas of your life are under the treacherous influence of the flesh? Honestly examine the results and risks of your sinful habits. Surrender those areas to the lordship of Christ.
3. What fruits of the Spirit (Gal. 5:22–23) are evident in your life? Which ones are lacking?

Additional Resources

Ezekiel 36:24–27; 37:14
John 15:1–5
Romans 8:1–17
2 Corinthians 5:14–17

Galatians 2:20
1 John 1:5–6; 2:15; 4:4

Henry Blackaby, *Experiencing the Cross* (Sisters, OR: Multnomah, 2005).

Henry Blackaby and Melvin Blackaby, *Experiencing the Resurrection* (Colorado Springs: Multnomah, 2008).

Roy Hession, *When I Saw Him: Where Revival Begins* (Fort Washington, PA: Christian Literature Crusade, 1975).

John Hunter, *Limiting God* (Grand Rapids, MI: Zondervan, 1966; reprint ed., Kingsport, TN: Fresh Springs Publications, 1995).

Andrew Murray, *Full Life in Christ* (Springdale, PA: Whitaker House, 1981).

Andrew Murray, *The Master's Indwelling* (Springdale, PA: Whitaker House, 1983).

Andrew Murray, *The Spirit of Christ* (Springdale, PA: Whitaker House, 1984).

James A. Stewart, *Heaven's Throne Gift* (Asheville, NC: Revival Literature: 1956).

A. W. Tozer, *The Divine Conquest* (Old Tappan, NJ: Fleming H. Revell Co., 1950).

How can I spend enough time with God when my schedule is already full?

Time is the most valuable resource business leaders have. How you choose to fill your calendar has profound implications. So, yes, giving time to God involves sacrifice, but it is the most meaningful offering you can bring to the altar as you worship him. Honoring God has a cost. Neglecting time with the Lord in favor of other pursuits is, in essence, idolatry. The hard truth is, when we do not have enough time for God, that says more about our view of God than our busy schedule.

It is illusory to think you will have more time later than you have now. Even retired people confess their lives get too busy for God. Now is the time to adjust your schedule. Extra time will not magically appear on your calendar. You have to be proactive and plan for time with your Lord.

A frequent question we hear is, how much is "enough" devotional time? The key is unhurried time with God. This allows for reading your Bible, pondering what you have read, praying, and listening to what God might say to you. If you are constantly checking your watch, you are obviously distracted and not experiencing unhurried time.

Unhurried time with God is the best time-saver of your day. Allow God to focus your mind on the things he knows are important. Let him prepare your heart for the challenges he knows you will face that day. Many business leaders have marveled that the Scriptures they read in the morning were exactly what they needed to know when a situation cropped up later that day. Christian businesspeople often share examples of how God strengthened them in the morning so they were prepared when the day held inevitable tests and difficulties. People who assume they are too busy to spend unhurried time with God underestimate how God will equip them to be at their best throughout their workday.

You may say, "But you don't know how busy I am!" The answer to that is, "You don't know the God you're going to meet!" We are not talking about a religious exercise. The God who fashioned the universe and created life itself wants to engage *you* in conversation. He is in the present as well as in the future, and he knows every detail of your life; so time spent with God is never wasted. Moreover, he gave up his only Son to suffer for your sins because he loves you with an infinite love.

Are you certain you are too busy for him?

People often lament that they are not morning people. Our response to that is, "Get over it!" If someone wanted to close a fabulous business deal and asked to meet with you for breakfast at 5:30 a.m., you would undoubtedly be there punctually and sporting a good attitude. What are the possibilities for your life every time God meets with you? He spoke and the earth came into existence (Gen. 1:6–7). God's Word brought the dead to life (John 11:43). Jesus' voice gave the blind their sight. The Lord spoke and sinners were transformed into saints (Mark 2:5). With a word, Jesus instantly stilled a storm (Matt. 8:26). What is the potential for your life every time God communicates with you? Is it worth getting up early for?

Jeremiah 7:13 describes an incredible moment. Almighty God claimed, "Because I have spoken to you time and time again but you wouldn't listen, and I have called to you, but you wouldn't answer . . ." It is inconceivable that Almighty God could be prepared to meet with us, then be stood up because we resent rising early to meet with him!

Here are some practical things you can do to make time to spend with your Lord:

- *Give up television.* It is bewildering how many Christians complain of their lack of time for God, but they religiously watch their favorite TV shows. Planning for unhurried time with God may mean you forego late night news programs so you are fresh and alert for God in the morning.
- *Aim for an early bedtime.* Avoid filling your mind with images, sounds, or issues that will resonate in your mind late into the night and into the morning, distracting you from focusing on God.
- *End your day with prayer.* Focus on God as you retire for the night. Ask him to give you rest, and offer to him the stresses and worries for the coming day.
- *Renounce the snooze button!* When the alarm goes off in the morning, get up!
- *Do whatever you need to do so you are awake and alert in the morning.* You may need to take a shower or have coffee before your time with God. There is no point in rising early to meet with God if you are comatose!
- *Audit your schedule and ruthlessly eliminate time wasters.* You can find various times to meet with God if you are intentional about it. While commuting to work, you can listen to the Bible and Christian devotionals on CD. You can read your Bible while traveling on a plane. Make technology work for you so you can study God's Word while you travel. Install Bible programs on your handheld, or biblical software on your laptop.
- *Try to schedule your day so the most pressing business is not early in your morning.* This will help allow unhurried time for prayer first thing in the day without having to fret about your first appointment.

- *Do not be drawn into frivolous, idle talk.* Hours can be wasted at work in meaningless conversations that, if the time had been used productively, would have allowed you more discretionary time with God.

There are numerous ways to free up time so you have more to offer the Lord. The bottom line is, you will give your time to what is most important to you. As you begin to spend unhurried time with the Lord, you will find it becoming a priority in your heart, not just on your calendar.

Questions for Reflection

1. How would you evaluate the current use of your time? Do you think it honors God?
2. What does your schedule reflect about your priorities?
3. How might you adjust your timetable so you can devote more unhurried time to God?
4. What activities and commitments could you give up so you have more time for God?

Additional Resources

Psalms 1:1–3; 25:4–5; 39:4; 40:1,8
Ephesians 5:16
Colossians 4:5
Revelation 1:3; 2:7, 29

Brother Lawrence, *The Practice of the Presence of God* (Springdale, PA: Whitaker House, 1982).
A. W. Tozer, *The Pursuit of God* (Harrisburg, PA: Christian Publications, 1948).

Andrew Murray, *Daily Experience with God* (Springdale, PA: Whitaker House, 1984).

Eugene Peterson, *A Long Obedience in the Same Direction* (Downers Grove, IL: InterVarsity Press, 1980).

Richard A. Swenson, *Margin: Restoring Emotional, Physical, Financial, and Time Reserves to Overloaded Lives* (Colorado Springs: NavPress, 1992).

Donald S. Whitney, *Simplify Your Spiritual Life: Spiritual Disciplines for the Overwhelmed* (Colorado Springs: NavPress, 2003).

Marjorie Dorr
Chief Strategy Officer (Retired)
Wellpoint, Inc.

A number of years ago, I was an executive in corporate America and was consumed with knowing God's will for my life. I wanted to know my bigger purpose besides my executive role. Unfortunately, more than I wanted a relationship with God, I wanted a road map for my future. I wanted God to tell me his big, hairy, audacious goal (BHAG) for my life, and then I would put together a plan, map it out, and complete the task.

That is not what Jesus did with his disciples, however. They weren't given a road map from Jesus; they were simply given an opportunity to walk with Jesus daily. This was profound for me—the simplicity of Matthew 4:17–20, where Jesus simply said, "Repent . . . follow me."

So I began my journey of following Jesus, beginning with "repent, follow me." I needed to turn around, to abandon my prior priorities. Sure, I claimed that God was my number-one priority, family number two, and work number three. But when I evaluated my calendar, this wasn't how I was living. I needed to elevate God—to see the incredible holiness of God—to stand in awe (actually, to lay on the ground in awe).

And at the moment of my repentance, the God of the universe invited me into a relationship with him.

He calls each of us to into a relationship with him, to follow him. It's not about what our purpose is in life (which is so amazingly egocentric). It's about surrendering to God, following him like the disciples did and doing his will. "This is eternal life," Jesus said, "that they may know You, the only true God, and the One You have sent—Jesus Christ" (John 17:3).

This is what you do when you love God with all your heart, with all your soul, and with all your mind (Matt. 22:37). You drop your own plans, your own purpose, your own will, and you choose to spend time with him, to get to know him. For me, a busy executive, this meant rising at 5 a.m. to spend unhurried time with the Lord daily. If God was my number-one priority, then I needed to act like it. But one of the challenges of spending time with God is that he might tell you to do something you don't want to do. As John 14:15 says, "If you love Me, you will keep my commandments."

Three years ago, God gave me a huge command: "Resign from being CEO (of Anthem Blue Cross Blue Shield NE) to spend more time with your family."

I had wrestled for a long time with knowing that my boys needed a different school environment and that my husband and I needed to spend more time together, as our jobs were requiring us to be away from home for long periods. But as logical as it was to resign, I struggled to pull the trigger.

When I finally had the conversation with my boss, he was incredibly supportive and shared with me his disappointments. He had actually hoped I would be a candidate to be his successor. (Momentarily, my ego began to flirt with the possibility of the promotion.) But I remained faithful to God's direction for my life.

God, being infinitely loving, truly had his hand in the process. My boss returned with an offer for me to work part-time as the chief strategy officer, allowing me to spend more time with God and my family while still having a significant ability to transform health care for the largest health plan in the country. I was thrilled! I hadn't previously considered this possibility.

My relationship with God grew as I worked fewer hours. It also showed me how much I had missed my family in the sixteen years of working sixty to eighty-hour work weeks. My boys had a limited understanding of God, and my marriage was weaker than I realized. Although I struggled with working part-time (I usually worked at least forty hours per week), I did spend more time unhurried with God most mornings, invested in my relationship with my husband, and taught my boys about God through our newly implemented morning devotions. But soon I heard God's voice again asking me to resign. Completely.

This time it didn't take me months of struggling and praying to understand. I immediately obeyed and trusted God. Although it took five months for me to finally transition my responsibilities, I am finally retired (for now) and at peace. I am grateful that I listened to God two years ago or I might have been offered (and accepted) the CEO job, since my boss announced his retirement simultaneously. But my spiritual maturity wasn't ready for the CEO position. I know that. It's highly likely that I would not have kept God my number-one priority. I would have simply squeezed him into my many priorities. I also know that my family would have suffered greatly because we didn't have a strong enough foundation.

I am still working on letting go of my busyness so that I can have time for solitude and my relationship with God, delighting in the Lord's instruction and meditating on it "day and night" (Ps. 1:2). I am learning to be still, to enjoy solitude more than being busy. Henri Nouwen wrote about the struggle that most of us type-A personalities have with drowning in activities and being over involved. He said, "By allowing the Lord to be in the center, life becomes simpler, more unified and more focused. . . . The goal is to live life less as an attempt to conquer new land and hold on to it, but more as a grateful response to the gifts of God."

I struggle with being drawn to many activities, wanting to conquer new land and help people around the world. God, however, has gently but clearly said to wait. I need to keep working with him and my family. I need to continue building a proper foundation.

So I am embracing solitude, ministering to my immediate family, my church, and my friends in ways I haven't previously. I am truly trying to lead like Jesus—spending time with the Father daily, mentoring the people around me, and joining God in the work I see him doing around me. To lead like Jesus, I have to spend time with Jesus, have a heart like Jesus, and really behave like Jesus. This is what is slowly influencing the people I interact with daily.

God is good.

MARJORIE DORR is a 23-year veteran of corporate America, having worked in such companies as Wellpoint and LaSalle Bank. She also holds an MBA from the University of Chicago and a BBA from the University of Iowa. Marjorie is involved with several not-for-profit organizations, including Lead Like Jesus, an organization cofounded by Ken Blanchard with a mission "to inspire and equip people to lead like Jesus." She and her husband, Len, make their home in Connecticut with their two boys.

PART 4

My Family Life

Can you be a successful leader if your family is fractured by broken relationships? The world says yes. The Bible, however, says no (1 Tim. 3:4–5). Keeping the family together has proven to be a huge challenge for many otherwise successful people. Some of the most famous business magnates in history were not even on speaking terms with their children; others could not translate their business success into marital harmony.

Working with business leaders, we observe that when God claims his rightful place in their lives, one of the first areas to fall under the Holy Spirit's conviction is family relationships (Mal. 2:13–14; 4:6). Our foremost human connection is with our spouse, followed by our relationship with our children. Business, church, and other social alliances all fall behind our primary relationships with our family.

Tragically, many executives forfeit the most precious relationships they have in order to get ahead. John D. Rockefeller became the wealthiest man of his day, yet all his influence, money, and persuasive skills could not convince his daughter Edith to visit him during his final decades. Too often, people neglect those things which matter most in order to pursue their careers. Tragically, they find themselves financially successful but personally dissatisfied. They foolishly forfeit the relationships that could have brought them joy and contentment.

Henry has participated in regular conference calls with Christian corporate CEOs for years. When these business leaders report on how they are doing, they don't focus on quarterly profits or market shares; they talk candidly about their marriages and families. They ask for prayer when their relationships are struggling. These leaders realize what truly matters. It is extremely encouraging to hear how God is healing wounded marriages and bringing reconciliation with formerly estranged children. Significantly, as of this writing, none of the CEOs we work with has suffered a divorce, despite the numerous pressures and temptations these leaders regularly face.

The following are several of the most common and challenging questions that business leaders ask us regarding their families.

How can I balance work and family?

This is a constant challenge for harried businesspeople. Work responsibilities are relentless. Busy professionals are perhaps the world's worst at convincing themselves they will give more attention to their neglected family once things at work settle down. Some people focus all their efforts on gaining a certain corporate position or reaching a particular income level before turning their full attention to their family. Then they discover to their dismay that they've lost their family in the process.

The quest for a balanced life has become popular in our culture. Busy people are regularly exhorted to strive for equilibrium in their lives. This means giving equal time and attention to each of their priorities. A businessman is urged to put in his eight hours at the office and then promptly arrive home in time for dinner, then coach his son's Little League baseball team and take his daughter to her riding lessons while going for a walk with his wife, maintaining his house and yard, and setting aside adequate time for exercise and attending a committee meeting at church. Inevitably, this quest for balance leads to frustration, not to mention exhaustion.

Our experience has been that life is rarely balanced. For that matter, the people we know who have been used by God to dramatically change their world have been noticeably imbalanced. Jesus was not balanced. At one point in his life, he spent forty days fasting and communing with his

Father. At other times, he was so pressed upon by the crowds who followed him that to be able to pray he would escape to a mountain, pray through the night, or rise up early in the morning (Mark 1:35; 6:46; Luke 6:12). Jesus could share a meal at times with his disciples (Luke 22:14–22). On other occasions, he would forego eating because he had more important things to do (John 4:32). Jesus would sometimes invite people to come to him to receive rest (Matt. 11:28). At other times, Jesus was so weary, even a life-threatening storm could not rouse him from his slumber (Matt. 8:24–25).

Jesus lived his life with passion but not necessarily with balance. Yet at the close of his life, he concluded, "I have glorified You on the earth by completing the work You gave Me to do" (John 17:4). Likewise, at his death Jesus triumphantly cried: "It is finished!" (John 19:30). What was his secret? He constantly sought his Father's agenda, and his Father consistently showed him what he should do that day (John 5:19–20, 30).

You must allow the Holy Spirit to guide you daily to know how to invest your time and effort. Each day may not be lived with perfect balance, but at the close of your life, you will discover you have accomplished everything God assigned you to do.

God will not lead you to neglect your family, your health, or your job. He expects you to be wise and to care for these things. But at times you may be uncertain whether to take a business trip or to stay home with your family. You'll have to decide whether to work late at the office or to attend a meeting at church. The Holy Spirit will guide you to know what you should do (John 14:16–18).

God is omniscient. He knows the future. He understands how to maximize your time so you are a good spouse, parent, career person, neighbor, and church member. God created you. He knows your responsibilities. He can lead you in a way that honors him and gives you abundant life (John 10:10).

God created marriage, the most intimate human relationship of all. He commanded us to make our spouses our top human priority (Gen. 2:24).

God condemned those who abused this love relationship and renounced their marital commitment (Mal. 2:13–16). God abhors adultery and detests divorce (Mal. 2:16). To neglect or to betray the sacred marriage bond is an offense to God.

When a marriage begins to falter, everything of value is in jeopardy. We've known people whose marriages were obviously disintegrating, but they did not adjust their schedule or priorities. We know pastors whose wives warned them they were struggling, but the pastors would not take time from "God's work" to heal the relationship or to seek counseling. When their marriage collapsed, so did their ministries.

You can be certain that if your marriage begins to show signs of strain, the Holy Spirit will prompt you to give that relationship your maximum attention. Incredibly, we have had distraught executives tell us their marriage was failing and they did not know what to do. Yet they could list all the successes they were having at work and recite the leadership they were giving to ministries in their church. They had not reduced their schedule or commitments in any significant way to invest more energy into their marriage. These people were experiencing failure and frustration at home while simultaneously soaking up success and accolades at work and at church. They naturally gravitated to the sources of their victory, but the cost was greater failure in their marriage. Some businesspeople bitterly complain that their company's excessive demands are injuring their family, but changing jobs is out of the question. This is strong evidence of misplaced priorities.

God expects us—in fact he *commands* us—to rear our children conscientiously with the ultimate goal that each one will love and honor him. The Bible bears heartbreaking witness to men and women who successfully led God's people or their nation but who failed miserably in influencing their own children. Eli was a long-serving priest whose children grew up to be corrupt and ignorant of the Lord (1 Sam. 2:12). Samuel's record in leading God's people was impeccable, but his two adult sons were unprincipled and immoral (1 Sam. 8:3). David, the brilliant military commander and king, floundered as a husband and father, suffering numerous painful consequences as a result. These were good men with the best of intentions; they accomplished great things. Yet they fell woefully short as parents.

Numerous biblical passages beseech us as parents to diligently teach our children God's truths (Deut. 6:7). These verses do not prescribe how many nights a week a parent should be at home or how often to volunteer at our child's school. The Scripture simply emphasizes that parents are to thoroughly instruct their children in God's ways (Prov. 22:6). We don't all have the same amount of time to spend with our children, but we are all commanded to teach them to walk with God (Ps. 78:4–7).

Back to the question of balancing work and family: the answer lies in the Holy Spirit's guidance. Let the Holy Spirit direct you.

Both of us travel a great deal. Yet we have taken seriously God's commands to teach our children to follow him. All five of Henry's children are in full-time Christian ministry. Richard's children—ages twenty-two, twenty, and seventeen—are all walking with the Lord. Neither of us is a parenting expert, and it has not been easy to be away from home so much. But we have both trusted the Holy Spirit to help us. God has blessed us incredibly and provided us many unique opportunities to lead our children in ways we could never have initiated on our own. He will do the same with you if you seek his help.

Questions for Reflection

1. List the priorities you know God has given you.
2. How is your life presently honoring these priorities?
3. Are you giving your marriage the attention it requires? Ask your spouse to help you answer this question!
4. What can be deleted from your schedule so you can properly respond to what God is asking you to do in your family?

Additional Resources

Psalms 78:1–8; 101:2–4; 127:1

Proverbs 3:19–23; 10:1; 13:24; 14:1; 15:5; 15:20; 20:7; 22:6; 23:24; 27:23; 29:15,17; 31:28

Henry Brandt and Kerry Skinner, *Marriage God's Way* (Nashville: Broadman & Holman, 1999).

Gary D. Chapman, *Covenant Marriage: Building Communication and Intimacy* (Nashville: Broadman & Holman, 2003).

James C. Dobson, *Love for a Lifetime: Building a Marriage that Will Go the Distance* (Portland: Multnomah, 1975).

Steve Farrar, *Point Man: How a Man Can Lead a Family* (Portland: Multnomah, 1990).

Gary Thomas, *Sacred Marriage* (Grand Rapids, MI: Zondervan, 2000).

Emerson Eggerichs, *Love and Respect: The Love She Most Desires, the Respect He Desperately Needs* (Nashville: Thomas Nelson, 2004).

How can I be a spiritual leader to my children when business constantly takes me away from home?

A busy schedule does not have to prevent you from leading your family wisely. Your presence or absence does not ultimately determine your domestic leadership. Rather, your leadership and guidance as a parent is based on your proven character and influence in your home whether you are frequently absent or not. As we mentioned earlier, the key is your relationship with God. If business does call for your frequent absence from home, it means you have to work purposefully to be the leader your family needs you to be.

Several biblical principles speak to this truth:

First, regardless of where your business travel or responsibilities take you, pray for and earnestly intercede for your children. Your kids ought to know that their parents diligently pray for them and expect God to work in their lives. Instead of spending the evening in your hotel room watching television, kneel by the bed and cry out to God for your spouse and children. Times away from home can be transformed into powerful moments of intercession for your family members.

Second, your leadership in your home flows out of your love relationship with God (Deut. 6:5). When you put God first in everything you do, he will honor you as you seek to lead your family (1 Sam. 2:30). There is no influence more powerful on children than parents who model a close walk with God.

Your children can discern whether you are merely religious or whether your relationship with Christ is your foremost priority. When you face a crisis, your family watches to see if you turn instinctively to the Lord. When you suffer a broken relationship, your children observe whether you earnestly and humbly seek reconciliation. Living out your intimate walk with God before your family is the most influential thing you can do as a spiritual leader in your home.

Absorb the Scriptures into your mind and heart, and strive to be obedient to everything God's Word says (Deut. 6:6; Josh. 1:7–8; Ps. 1). The key is not that you *believe* God's Word but that you *practice* it. Your family will not be impressed by your belief that the Bible commands people to love their enemies. They will, however, be impacted when they see you obey Scripture and love *your* enemies. The important thing is not how many Scripture verses you can quote to your children when they do wrong but how many Scripture verses your kids see you living out before them.

Third, diligently teach your children what God's Word says (Deut. 6:7). Parents pass along numerous nuggets of their own wisdom. How much more important to teach our children to search the Scriptures to find *God's* wisdom! We have tried to faithfully share with our families what God is teaching us. We have also encouraged our children to pursue their own daily walk with God.

Therefore, guide your children to know how to study God's Word. There are numerous devotional guides geared for children, teens, and young adults. Do not leave spiritual instruction solely up to your children's Sunday school teachers or youth workers. Take responsibility for seeing that your kids thoroughly absorb biblical truths as well as God's promises.

Teaching your family to know and discern God's ways can happen in any setting. Throughout the day and week, you can guide your family spiritually. Deuteronomy 6:7 says to teach your children whenever you're at home, when you're out and about, or as you drive them to school or to their baseball game. Sometimes it's possible to take a child or your whole family on a trip with you. Capitalize on these occasions and use them wisely. All parents—but *especially* parents who travel on business—must seize opportunities to talk with their families about God's will and his ways.

Sometimes late at night is when young people tend to open up and share their hearts. While a breakfast meeting might be more convenient for their busy dad, a bedtime chat could lead to a meaningful spiritual encounter. Many of the greatest teaching moments in our children's lives have come at the most ordinary moments: while driving in the car together, when a teenager flopped on our bed at midnight, during a meal or standing around the island in the kitchen having an evening snack. Often, when dad is away, these conversations take place by phone, e-mail, or text message.

God said that what we hold in our hands will instruct our children (6:8). When our children look at us and what occupies our time, they have a sermon preached to them. If parents are frequently holding the computer mouse or TV remote control but never their Bible, the message comes through clearly. Children who see their mom and dad racing home to their golf clubs but not having time for their family understand what is important to their parents.

Finally, Deuteronomy 6:9 says to "write [God's Word] on the doorposts of your house and on your gates." The way you decorate, arrange, and use your home tells your children much about your view of God. Some people see their home as an investment. Others use it as a means of ministry. Some houses are like museums filled with precious artifacts. Other homes are a hub of Christian activity where love abounds. Some adorn their walls with the latest artistic decor. Others fill their rooms with visual reminders of God's goodness. Choose to display Scriptures in your house, and tell your children why those verses are meaningful to you. Every room can hold the message of a special verse, prayer, or object of spiritual significance.

A great exercise for parents is to claim each promise found in Psalm 78 for your family. Be a leader in your home at each moment available to you. Place classic devotional books and Christian biographies into your children's hands. Invite godly people, missionaries, and ministers into your home so your children are exposed to strong Christians. Be sure to involve your family in a local church. If your teens belong to a strong youth group and your spouse has supportive Christian friends, your time away from home will not be as hard on your family. Be careful never to criticize your pastoral staff or congregation before your family. You will be planting destructive seeds in their hearts that will ripen into apostasy when your children become teenagers and adults. Strive to model Christlikeness to your children. They may not remember every word you said as they were growing up, but the model of your life will be unforgettable.

There are numerous ways to stay closely connected with your family, even while you're away. Cell phones, e-mail, text messaging, and Webcams make it possible to provide spiritual leadership to your home even when you're on the road. You don't have to drop off the face of the earth when you go on a business trip! Make every effort to talk with your spouse each day and to keep up on what's happening in your children's lives. E-mail your kids or get online with them. Calls and e-mails may seem like small talk, but you are staying involved in the everyday life of your family. Then you're not a stranger when you arrive home. Keep in mind that what may seem trivial to you from afar may matter a great deal to your spouse or your child. Be sure to keep track of important events in your family's lives and be involved in those occasions from where you are. If you have to miss your daughter's piano recital, have flowers and a note delivered to her on that day. Schedule a date to sit with her and watch the video of her performance together after you return home. Send Scriptures by e-mail. We know one man who prayed with his daughter every night at bedtime, whether he was on the road or not. Staying involved in your family's spiritual life may take some creativity when you travel, but your family will appreciate and benefit from the effort.

Questions for Reflection

1. What challenges do you face in providing spiritual leadership to your family?
2. List some ways you could play a more active role in your family's spiritual lives. What adjustments will these require from you?
3. How could you maintain better contact with your family when you have to travel?

Additional Resources

Proverbs 17:6
Malachi 4:5–6
Ephesians 5:22–33
Colossians 3:18–21
1 Peter 3:7

Henry Blackaby and Marilynn Blackaby, *Experiencing God as Couples* (Nashville: LifeWay Press, 2000).

Henry Blackaby and Richard Blackaby, *Experiencing God: Collegiate Edition* (Nashville: LifeWay Press, 2005).

Henry Blackaby and Richard Blackaby, *Spiritual Leadership: Moving People on to God's Agenda* (Nashville: Broadman & Holman, 2001).

Henry Blackaby and Richard Blackaby, *TQ 120 A, B, and C* (Nashville: Broadman & Holman, 2005).

Henry Blackaby and Richard Blackaby, *When God Speaks: Youth Edition* (Nashville: LifeWay Press, 1997).

Henry Blackaby and Richard Blackaby, *Discovering God's Daily Agenda* (Nashville: Thomas Nelson, 2004).

Gary Chapman, *Covenant Marriage: Building Communication and Intimacy* (Nashville: Broadman & Holman, 2003).

Steve Farrar, *Point Man: How a Man Can Lead a Family* (Portland: Multnomah, 1990).

Gary Smalley and John Trent, *The Blessing* (Nashville: Thomas Nelson, 1986).

How can I protect my marriage when the world around me is constantly assaulting it?

You are courting disaster if you do not actively and aggressively protect yourself from any form of unfaithfulness to your spouse. This world is relentlessly hostile to your Christian commitments, and Satan will destroy your marriage if he can. A lawyer's billboard advertises with these cynical words: "Life is short. Get a divorce."

But Scripture is clear: "Be sober! Be on the alert! Your adversary the Devil is prowling around like a roaring lion, looking for anyone he can devour" (1 Pet. 5:8). If you are not tenacious to safeguard the most precious human relationship in your life, you are, to put it bluntly, a fool (Prov. 5:22–23).

Our society is obsessed with sex. You cannot turn on the television, go to a movie, look at a billboard, or check the Internet without having sex thrust into your face. Hollywood winks at and even glamorizes adultery. Advertisers want you to feel like a loser if you cannot immediately gratify every desire. In such a carnal climate, it is not easy to maintain purity in your deeds and thoughts. The office can present numerous temptations as men and women work together all day while separated from their spouses. Business travel can leave people exhausted, lonely, and vulnerable to temptation. But here are a few suggestions to help you remain wholly committed to your spouse despite the pressures of work and travel:

1. Be assured that God hates divorce (Mal. 2:16). He is determined that what he has put together, no one will separate (Mark 10:9). God is deeply concerned that you do everything possible to protect your marriage. As with every temptation you face, God will provide a means of escape from the factors that threaten your marriage (1 Cor. 10:13). Therefore, there is no excuse for allowing your marriage to succumb to immorality.

2. Recognize that Satan is hostile to your marriage. Scripture calls Satan the "prince of the power of the air" (Eph. 2:2 NASB). This world is permeated with his evil influence. And nowhere is this more evident than in media. Hollywood mocks your Christian values and concerns. It flaunts every manner of depravity. It thrusts pornographic images into your face. The media can fill your mind with impure, idolatrous, and evil images. If you do not guard what you watch, you are inviting adulterous thoughts to pour into your mind.

Scripture warns that adultery begins in the heart. Jesus cautioned: "For from within, out of people's hearts, come evil thoughts, sexual immoralities, thefts, murders, adulteries, greed, evil actions, deceit, lewdness, stinginess, blasphemy, pride, and foolishness. All these evil things come from within and defile a person" (Mark 7:21–23). Jesus also declared: "But I tell you, everyone who looks at a woman to lust for her has already committed adultery with her in his heart" (Matt. 5:28).

Christians who seek to protect the purity of their marriage relationship will meticulously block adulterous thoughts and images from creeping into their minds. People who watch movies filled with blatant and suggestive sex and yet believe it will not affect them or their marriage are deceiving themselves and dishonoring their spouses. You've heard Christians claim that a certain movie has a great story if you can get past the sex and profanity. The problem is, you can't get past it. Scripture exhorts us to look only upon that which is pure and good (Phil. 4:8). Job made a covenant with his eyes not to look lustfully upon another woman (Job 31:1). The psalmist declared: "I will not set anything godless before my eyes. I hate the doing of transgressions; it will not cling to me" (Ps. 101:3). The psalmist also prayed: "Test me, LORD, and try me; examine my heart and mind" (Ps. 26:2). Christians must be extremely protective of what enters their minds and hearts. Jesus said that to lust after someone else is to commit the sin of adultery. Every lustful thought you allow to linger in your mind is a sin against God and your spouse.

3. *Take active steps to protect yourself from any form of impropriety.* You may choose never to watch television while in a hotel on business travel. Richard habitually places a picture of Lisa and the children on top of the TV in the hotel room and leaves the set turned off as a reminder of his family commitments. It is prudent to avoid being alone with a person of the opposite gender. If your job calls for you to interact with someone from the opposite sex, you should be careful to meet in public places or to invite a colleague to join you. For a Christian, suggestive humor, off-color jokes, or inappropriate teasing with people of the opposite sex is out of bounds. We know people who claimed their suggestive teasing in the workroom was innocent fun, only to discover (as is always the case) that what had been coming out of their mouths reflected what was in their hearts (Matt. 12:34–35).

4. *Surround yourself with people to whom you are accountable.* The most important person in this endeavor ought to be your spouse. Keep your marriage partner aware of who you work with and what your job assignments involve. Involve your spouse in the process of hiring anyone with whom you will work closely. Don't keep secrets. If your spouse is uneasy about the intentions of one of your colleagues, take those concerns seriously. Be sure to have at least one prayer/accountability partner who prays for you and who asks you the hard questions. Most people who fall into immorality had no system of accountability in their lives. If you truly want to protect your marriage, accountability is a must.

5. *Meditate on the consequences of adultery.* While Hollywood makes infidelity appear commonplace, natural, and exciting, Scripture is graphically clear about the pain and devastation it causes (Prov. 5:7–14). We have both counseled victims of adultery. We have seen up-close that the pain is unfathomable, and the anguish the children experience is lifelong. Don't be deceived into thinking it is just a game or a passing fling. The consequences of such a sin are so horrendous that godly men and women ought to shudder at the thought.

6. *Continually nurture your love relationship with your husband or wife.* Proverbs urges us to find our sexual satisfaction with our spouses (Prov. 5:15). Scripture commands husbands to lay their lives down for their wives (Eph. 5:25). A lifelong marriage partner is a precious gift from God, someone to be cherished and deeply loved. No sacrifice is too great to preserve the purity of the marriage relationship. Declining to watch TV, go to a movie, or meet with a colleague for dinner is a small price to pay to protect your marriage. The best defense against adultery is a close walk with God and a vibrant relationship with your spouse.

Questions for Reflection

1. What strict and thorough safeguards have you built into your life to protect you from sexual immorality?
2. What additional boundaries is God leading you to build into your life?
3. How are you aggressively protecting your mind from viewing or listening to things that are immoral or unbecoming to a Christian?
4. What might you do to strengthen your relationship with your spouse?

Additional Resources

Genesis 2:24
Psalms 37:4–5, 37–38
Matthew 5:27–30; 6:22–23; 15:19–20; 19:1–10
1 Corinthians 3:16; 6:19–20; 10:13; 13
Ephesians 5:22–33
Colossians 3:18–19

Henry Blackaby, *Holiness: God's Plan for Fullness of Life* (Nashville: Thomas Nelson, 2003).

Henry Blackaby, *Experiencing the Cross: Your Greatest Opportunity for Victory over Sin* (Sisters, OR: Multnomah, 2005).

Henry Blackaby and Claude King, *Fresh Encounter: Experiencing God through Prayer, Humility, and a Heartfelt Desire to Know Him* (Nashville: Broadman & Holman, 1996).

Henry Blackaby and Norman Blackaby, *Called and Accountable: Discovering Your Place in God's Eternal Purpose* (Birmingham, AL: New Hope Publishers, 2005).

Lois Mowday Rabey, *The Snare: Understanding Emotional and Sexual Entanglements* (Colorado Springs: NavPress, 1988).

Steve Farrar, *Finishing Strong: Finding the Power to Go the Distance* (Sisters, OR: Multnomah, 1995).

What do I do if my spouse is not walking with the Lord and doesn't support me as a spiritual leader?

One of the most heart-wrenching issues in our ministry with business-people concerns those who did not begin their marriage walking closely with the Lord. As a result, they married unbelievers, or they did not lead their families to make God a priority. Then later, when they earnestly began to follow God, their spouse did not share their enthusiasm. To the revived Christian's dismay, their faith actually put a wedge in their marriage and family. It is agonizing for these sincere Christians to watch their families ignoring God and embracing the world's values. They bear the burdensome knowledge that they are largely responsible for the disinterest in God that permeates their home. After all, for years they modeled the same behavior.

If you are presently struggling in this situation, here are some things to keep in mind:

1. Realize that your most important earthly relationship is the bond with your spouse. In years past, you may have allowed your business career to harm your marriage, relegating it to a backseat position on your list of priorities. Don't let your newfound love for God now injure it any further. Be very careful about this. People sometimes rediscover God and enthusiastically throw themselves into leading Bible studies and spending hours each week serving in their church while leaving their unbelieving spouses neglected at home. These people then grow frustrated with their lukewarm or unbelieving spouses.

God was a witness at your marriage ceremony. He does not want any marriage to end in failure. He loves your spouse more than you do. While God will expect your first loyalty to be to him, he will not lead you to do things that will destroy your marriage. He will not direct you to neglect your spouse. God knows that once you begin following him wholeheartedly, your next responsibility is to encourage your spouse to follow Christ fervently as well. You cannot abandon this responsibility in your eagerness to serve God in your church or community.

2. *Be careful to distinguish between your relationship with God and your commitment to your church.* The two are not identical. Loyalty to Christ does not mean you must live at your church. If your spouse is not yet walking with God, your being at every church function could damage your marriage. Spend time daily with God, but do not race off too far ahead of your life partner in your religious activity. Be prudent in your church commitments, especially before your spouse is prepared to serve with you or at least to be supportive. People have asked, "If my wife/husband will not go with God, should I go on alone?" God would never ask you to abandon your spouse in your effort to serve him. Your first ministry will be to your unbelieving spouse.

Be patient! It may have taken you a long time to return to the Lord. Give your spouse the benefit of time to also come to God. Each person has unique issues, questions, and struggles. Allow God to do a special work in your spouse's life just as he did in yours. Offer yourself as a friend with an open heart and a listening ear along your spouse's journey. The love of your life is worth waiting for!

3. The most important thing you can do right now is to pray. Your spouse has seen you at your worst. Your family may have watched you for years when you were not serious about God. You may have lost credibility when it comes to living the Christian life. Sometimes the people most resistant to your newfound faith are those who have known you best. You cannot erase your history, but you can ask the Holy Spirit to convince your spouse of the authenticity of your faith. Allow God to break down barriers to belief in your family just as he did with you. Ask God to show you what your part should be in bringing your family to him. God may give you an active role. Or he may lead you to pray and watch for his answer. Do not try to usurp the Holy Spirit's role in your family's life. Resist the urge to preach and convict! We know people who longed to see their family come to know Christ, but they inadvertently drove them away from God through their insensitivity and judgmental words.

It is difficult but not impossible to lead your family even without your spouse's support (2 Tim. 1:5). Your greatest influence upon your children may be the changed life they witness in you. If your children are young, it may mean taking them to church on your own. It will include praying with them and discussing spiritual truths with them. If your children are older, spend quality time with each one, sharing with them your pilgrimage of faith and what Christ means to you. Here again, Christian mentors from your church can become involved to help minister to your family so they see the love of Christ through others, too. Never be too proud to ask for help from your church family.

Above all, trust God to guide you. He cherishes your family. He is actively pursuing each of them. Offer your life as God's instrument to reach each of your family members. Don't grow discouraged and don't give up! Always believe that God can use you to make a difference in the spiritual lives of those you love.

Questions for Reflection

1. How are you presently exerting a spiritual influence upon your family?
2. How is your spouse responding to your spiritual leadership? What does that response tell you?
3. Do you sense God leading you to make adjustments in the way you relate to your family? If so, what will you change?
4. How are you praying for your family? How is God answering those prayers?

Additional Resources

Matthew 7:24–29
Ephesians 5:22–6:4
Colossians 3:18–21; 4:6
1 Timothy 5:8
1 Peter 3:1–7

Henry Blackaby and Richard Blackaby, *Spiritual Leadership: Moving People on to God's Agenda* (Nashville: Broadman & Holman, 2001).

Henry Blackaby and Tom Blackaby, *The Man God Uses* (Nashville: Broadman & Holman, 1999).

Steve Farrar, *Point Man: How a Man Can Lead a Family* (Portland: Multnomah, 1990).

Devotionals and Studies for Young People

Henry Blackaby and Claude King, *Experiencing God: Preteen Edition* (Nashville: LifeWay Press, 2005).

Henry Blackaby and Richard Blackaby, *Experiencing God: Collegiate Edition* (Nashville: LifeWay Press, 2005).

Henry Blackaby and Richard Blackaby, *When God Speaks: Youth Edition* (Nashville: LifeWay Press, 1997).

Henry Blackaby and Richard Blackaby, *TQ 120 A, B, and C* (Nashville: Brodman & Holman, 2005).

What do I do if my marriage seems to be broken beyond repair?

Marriage is too frequently a casualty in the lives of preoccupied businesspeople. The heavy demands on executives' lives, coupled with the worldly environment that engulfs them, puts a strain on marital relationships. God will sometimes awaken businesspeople to the weak spiritual condition in their home, but just as they begin to respond and to follow Christ, their spouse pulls back, giving up on the marriage. The situation looks hopeless. Other executives have become Christians, and their abrupt lifestyle change bewildered their unbelieving spouses, causing them to want out of the marriage. Marriages can suffer assault on many fronts. If your relationship with your spouse is in a perilous position, here are some thoughts that may help:

First, God hates divorce (Mal. 2:16). God does not despise divorcees, but he knows the agonizing consequences of a marriage breakup, and he understands the devastating effects on children, whom he desires to be "godly offspring." God will lead you to do everything possible to avert the breakup of your marriage. If your relationship with your spouse is in peril, know that you have Almighty God himself powerfully working to restore your union.

Second, the Christian's essential calling is to facilitate reconciliation (2 Cor. 5:18). The miracle of God's reconciliation with you compels you to draw others to Christ, too. For a Christian marriage to flourish, both persons must be committed to Christ. Your prayers and your efforts should be toward that end.

To bring about reconciliation with your spouse, first make sure you are right with God yourself. To be of use to God, you must deny yourself (Matt. 16:24). If you stubbornly defend your rights and affirm yourself before your spouse, you are not paying the price required to be reunited. Because of what Christ has done for us, we no longer live for ourselves but for him (2 Cor. 5:15). A marriage cannot thrive if both parties adamantly protect their own interests. Only when you give and forgive unconditionally will Christ's love flow unimpeded through you. The key is not changing your spouse but allowing Christ to transform you so he can use you to restore harmony in your marriage.

Third, understand that the primary problem in a floundering marriage is not miscommunication, unmet expectations, or financial and time pressures. It is sin. Sin is the root of every problem. Sin offends God (Ps. 51:4), drawing us away from him and turning our attention to other things—our pleasures, ambitions, pride, and hurt feelings. When we sin against God, we refuse his blessing and block out his guidance. Sin alienates us from others because it fosters selfishness, pride, envy, and greed. In a marriage relationship, which by nature is one of union, sin causes division, competitiveness, and hostility. Sin in any form is corrosive to a marriage.

Much of today's marriage counseling focuses on symptoms. Angry words, selfishness, and unfaithfulness are manifestations of sin left breeding in a person's heart. If a couple only addresses their communication problems, they will end up as two sinful, selfish people who are better at communicating. The key to restoring a marriage is *spiritual*. If you are seeking healing for your marriage, repent of the sin in your life and encourage your spouse to draw closer to the Lord as well. It may amaze you to see how many marital problems are resolved once a husband and wife both begin walking closely with the Lord.

Perhaps you are the one seeking to end your marriage. Have you been so deeply hurt that you have lost hope? Consider how much God forgave you. Read the Old Testament book of Hosea. There God said that sin and apostasy against him were as agonizing as adultery. Yet God could not let his people go. He relentlessly pursued them despite their rejection of him (Hos. 2:14–23). God expects us to demonstrate that same love and forgiveness, even if our spouse has deeply hurt us.

Your husband or wife may have gravely wounded you, and you feel as if the pain will never heal. From a human perspective, it will seem impossible to forgive. Yet God's love is boundless. When he fills your life with his love, you are empowered to absolve even the deepest hurt (Matt. 18:21–35). The love that enabled Jesus to cry out, "Father, forgive them!" as the brutal Roman soldiers nailed him to a cross will also help you forgive your spouse. God can fill your life with his peace to withstand a hostile attack or cold rejection (Phil. 4:6–7). Don't allow bitterness to incapacitate you. Don't retreat into a corner, dwelling on your victim status. Choose to love your life partner with Christ's love, and watch God do his divine work in your marriage. Just as God never gave up on you, don't ever give up on your marriage.

Finally, don't be ashamed to ask people to pray for you. Many marriages languish in silence because people are reluctant to tell anyone what is happening. Mobilize wise, godly friends to pray. There is incredible power in prayer. Saving your marriage is worth the humility it takes to enlist people to intercede on your behalf.

Questions for Reflection

1. Are there indications that your marriage is in peril? If so, what are the signs? Do you think God considers your situation hopeless?

2. Is your life characterized by forgiveness? What is the evidence? Are you beseeching God to pour out his loving forgiveness through you?
3. Have you grown bitter? If so, what can you do to be set free from the bondage of resentment?

Additional Resources

Hosea 2:14–3:5
Malachi 2:13–16
Matthew 5:43–48; 18:21–35
Mark 9:23
Romans 8:26, 31–39
1 Corinthians 7:10–16

Henry Blackaby and Marilynn Blackaby, *Experiencing God as Couples* (Nashville: LifeWay Press, 2000).
Melvin Blackaby, *Going the Second Mile: Letting God Take You Beyond Yourself* (Sisters, OR: Multnomah: 2006).
Richard Blackaby, *Putting a Face on Grace: Living a Life Worth Passing On* (Sisters, OR: Multnomah, 2006).
Henry Brandt and Kerry Skinner, *Marriage God's Way* (Nashville: Broadman & Holman, 1999).
Gary Chapman, *Covenant Marriage: Building Communication and Intimacy* (Nashville: Broadman & Holman, 2003).
Gary Thomas, *Sacred Marriage* (Grand Rapids, MI: Zondervan, 2000).
Emerson Eggerichs, *Love and Respect: The Love She Most Desires, the Respect He Desperately Needs* (Nashville: Thomas Nelson, 2004).

If I wasn't a godly parent for my children when they were young, how can I change things now?

Businesspeople often tenaciously pursue wealth, power, and reputation; then having achieved those goals, they finally turn their attention to their family. To their chagrin, they realize they have badly overlooked the most important people in their lives. Now they are desperately trying to make up for lost time. This is a tragic situation for a family to be in. If you were negligent as a Christian parent when your children were young, you will sorely need God's divine intervention.

According to the Bible, the time to lead your children to follow God is when they are young (Prov. 22:6). By the time they conclude their teen years, their values and beliefs are generally in place. They may have watched you idolize money for years. They may have heard you give lip service to Christ's lordship while you pursued your own goals and dreams. They may have seen you exploit people for your own gain as you lived a self-centered life. If you set an unchristlike example during your children's formative years, it will be hard to convince them not to do as you have done. But the great miracle of the Christian life is that with God, there is always hope.

Here are several truths to consider:

1. It is God who must convince your children of his love for them, not you. God will invite each of your children into a love relationship with him. Your responsibility is to be God's servant and to join him in this activity. Take heed: you cannot convince anyone of spiritual truth. Only the Holy Spirit can do that (Matt. 16:17; John 5:19–20; 6:44). Seek the Lord and ask him what your role in the process should be.

2. Remember there is no more powerful testimony to the reality of God's power than a changed life. A woman in Jesus' day had been divorced five times and was currently living with a man. She was not exactly an authority on righteous living. Yet when she encountered Christ, her transformation was so astounding that people who knew her reputation had to conclude something miraculous had occurred (John 4:39). Likewise, the greatest single thing you can do to convince your children that God is real is to let God totally transform *your* life. When Jesus walked on earth, sinners were naturally drawn to him. There was something about him they found irresistible. The more you become like Christ, the more appealing your testimony for him will be. Take time to share with your children what Christ has done in you. Don't force your faith on your family. Simply bear witness to what God has done in your heart. Allow the Holy Spirit to speak through your transformed life directly to your family.

3. Pray diligently for your children. Prayer is our lifeline (James 5:16–18). Prayer adjusts our lives to God's activity. Praying for your children will sharpen your spiritual senses so you recognize God's activity in their lives. As you pray, the Holy Spirit will help you discern how to reach your son or daughter's heart. Don't underestimate the power of prayer in *any* situation!

4. Understand that God may use other believers to get through to your children. Enlist the aid of wise friends and godly relatives. Don't be too proud to ask your church to intercede for your children's salvation. We know of one entire adult Bible study in which every member had a wayward child. As they prayed together each week for their children, that class saw every prodigal return to God! Due to your former lifestyle, your credibility with your children may be so damaged that despite your love and concern for them, you are not the primary one to lead them to Christ. But there may be someone else who can have a profound spiritual impact on your children. Be open and watchful for such a person.

As we were bringing up our children, we attempted to surround them with godly people they respected. Our teens spent time around believers who were keen on sports or hunting; they interacted with college students and young couples who were a lot of fun and dedicated to Christ. We tried to bring successful, godly leaders from all walks of life around our family. These people might say the same things we had repeatedly told our children, but somehow—coming from *them*—the truth resonated better. Sometimes an accomplished athlete or musician will find an audience that we might not get with our children. Find people who will reach out to your children and testify to the reality of God in unique ways.

5. *Be patient.* Allow your family the time to verify the transformation in your life so they know it's not a fleeting fad. Your son or daughter may have to experience the emptiness of pursuing worldly pleasures. Allow your children to develop their own unique relationship with God; they cannot live on your faith. You will naturally be eager for everyone in your family to know Christ as you do, but they must come to know him and love him in a way that is personal and meaningful to them. Then their faith will be genuine and not an act merely to please you.

Nothing is more precious to parents than the eternal salvation of their children. You should take this matter extremely seriously, but you must trust God to take the lead in reaching your family. God knows what he's doing. Confidently place your family in his hands.

Questions for Reflection

1. What do you think is preventing your children from following Christ?
2. How has your lifestyle hindered your children from believing in and following Christ?
3. What specifically is God asking you to do to help your children come to God?
4. How might you enlist other believers to help you in reaching your children for Christ?

Additional Resources

2 Corinthians 3:5; 5:20; 12:9
Galatians 2:20; 6:7–10
Ephesians 4:29; 6:4
Philippians 1:6; 2:12–13; 3:12–14; 4:13
Colossians 3:21; 4:6
James 5:16

Henry Blackaby and Richard Blackaby, *Spiritual Leadership: Moving People on to God's Agenda* (Nashville: Broadman & Holman, 2001).

Henry Blackaby and Tom Blackaby, *The Man God Uses* (Nashville: Broadman & Holman, 1999).

Steve Farrar, *Point Man: How a Man Can Lead His Family* (Portland: Multnomah, 1990).

John Beckett
Chairman
R. W. Beckett Corporation

I have found that being summoned to God's work can involve resisting that which threatens his work. I received such a "summons" in 1993 in the early stages of the modern work/faith movement.

A government regulatory body, the Equal Employment Opportunity Commission (EEOC), had issued guidelines regulating religious expression or display in the workplace. While these guidelines were at best intended to reduce religious discrimination, attorneys who examined the proposals concluded they could have a chilling effect on the most common and widely practiced forms of religious expression, like wearing religious jewelry to work or having a Bible on your desk. In fact, a major airline, anticipating the guidelines would soon take effect, had already notified employees that its bulletin boards could no longer be used for any postings with religious content.

I became aware of the EEOC's proposal days before the period for public comment was scheduled to end. I wrote the EEOC and encouraged a few business associates to write, but our letters of objection amounted to a trickle. Too little, too late. It was then I learned the period for comment remained open for existing and former members of Congress. I contacted a friend and former U.S. congressman who agreed to assist in an effort to overturn the guidelines.

For a few weeks, I smugly thought I had neatly delegated this project. But then I sensed a strong nudge from the Lord: "John, I want you to be the point person on this." I fussed, but I couldn't duck. I had to be fully involved. The next months would involve working closely to build a national coalition, meeting with lobbyists and legal counsel, even going face to face with the EEOC in Washington, DC.

The issue became highly visible, including coverage by major TV networks. The small trickle of letters became a great flood, exceeding 100,000—ten times the number previously received by the EEOC on any other issue. Momentum built in Congress, and some six months after our efforts began, a vote was taken in the U.S. Senate to withhold funding from the EEOC to promulgate these guidelines. By a miracle that I still cannot fully fathom, that vote was 100 to 0!

God gave grace that day to every working American, preserving for each of us the freedom to bring our faith to work in tangible and visible ways. How grateful I am that he allowed me—insisted, in fact—that I become involved.

JOHN BECKETT, upon his father's death in 1965, became the president and CEO of a small, family-owned manufacturing business—R. W. Beckett Corporation. He is now the chairman of the company and has helped guide the business to worldwide leadership in the manufacturing and sale of engineered components for residential and commercial heating. In 1999, the Christian Broadcasting Network named him "Christian Businessman of the Year," and he was named manufacturing "Entrepreneur of the Year" by Ernst & Young in 2003. He has also authored two books, *Loving Monday* and *Mastering Monday,* on how to practically integrate faith in the workplace. He holds a bachelor's degree in economics and mechanical engineering from MIT. He and his wife, Wendy, have six children and fifteen grandchildren.

PART 5

My Church and Community Life

The church is under attack. Critics loudly proclaim its irrelevance. This generation has the largest number of unchurched Americans in history. So, obviously, even though the church has existed for two thousand years, its purpose is still largely misunderstood. With so many denominations and forms of church government, organized religion can be a mystery even to believers. To outsiders, the church can often seem downright archaic.

Yet God loves the church. Christ laid down his life for it (Eph. 5:25). He is building the church (Matt. 16:18), and he is its Head (Col. 1:18). Therefore, anything Christ values so much ought to be important to us, as well.

For many Christian businesspeople, however, the church is an enigma. It is sometimes poorly administered and seems directionless. Some church leaders feel threatened by successful businesspeople. Those who thrive in the world of productivity, efficiency, and deadlines may find the operation of the church puzzling or even exasperating. To executives whose time is valuable and who expect large returns on their investment, the local church can become a place of frustration rather than fulfillment.

In our work with CEOs, we hear numerous questions from men and women who are unsure how they fit in to their local church. The following is a sampling of what they have asked us.

How should I invest myself in my church?

Christian businesspeople face unique challenges as they seek to find their place in their local church. If you are a successful businessperson, you may feel that your substantial tithe is contribution enough, so you need not serve in a ministry position. God, however, has equipped you with skills that could benefit his kingdom, and he wants you to place *everything* in your life at his disposal.

Have you considered why God added you to your church body? You may have based your decision on location, worship style, or the minister's preaching; but God knew where he wanted you to belong. He has equipped you with various skills, experiences, and passions that could uniquely benefit your church. But if you merely sit back and choose not to become involved, both you and your church will miss out on what God might have done through your service as a member.

God adds members to the church body as it pleases him (1 Cor. 12:18). While every church is obligated to carry out the Great Commission that Jesus elaborated before returning to heaven (Matt. 28:18–20), God also has specific assignments for each congregation. Moreover, each church is uniquely designed to fulfill its divine mandate. If God wants a church to be involved in medical missions, for example, he may equip the church with medical professionals as members. If God wants a church to reach the local university, he will equip the church with college students and faculty members who have a burden to reach the campus.

Since businesspeople are usually good at administration or finance, those are often the church committees to which they gravitate. No one is one-dimensional, however. You have other gifts completely unrelated to your career. And your church is the ideal place to channel those passions. In Richard's church, some of the people who find great joy in teaching Sunday school to preschoolers and school-aged children are engineers, geologists, and bankers. God may want to nudge you into a new and unanticipated area where you can grow spiritually. Perhaps God wants you to work with the youth or the elderly or to lead out in a Friday morning prayer time. He may give you a burden to spend some vacation time on a mission trip with your family or a group from your church.

We know one church whose membership included several chartered accountants. Not surprisingly, they were all placed on the church finance committee. But after the church went through the study *Experiencing God*, the entire committee resigned. They announced, "The church asked us to serve on the finance committee because our training is in finance. But we have been trained to take a conservative approach to budgeting. Our education has predisposed us to avoid walking by faith. Yet God says without faith, it is impossible to please him." The committee suggested that rather than only enlisting accountants to serve on the finance committee, the church should primarily find people who knew how to walk by faith.

Business leaders by nature are industrious men and women. They may be so preoccupied with weighty projects that they feel too busy to serve their local congregation. To some executives, traveling on international business trips or consummating multimillion dollar deals seems far more significant than chaperoning a youth mission trip or taking a shift in the church nursery. In truth, however, there is no greater investment one can make than in the kingdom of God.

People are eternal. Businesses are not.

Both of us travel a great deal. It is a rare treat to be in our own church on a Sunday. We can't take on a weekly responsibility at our churches, but God has blessed us both with areas to serve and to encourage our pastoral staff despite our schedules. God will show you how you can do that, too.

Prosperous professionals can be an intimidating influence in a congregation. Ministers may be highly educated and gifted communicators, but they are not always strong leaders. They have a shepherd's heart, and they would lay down their life for their flock; but for the life of them, some can't run an efficient committee meeting! Organizational deficiencies in a church are readily discerned by a businessperson. Often the area of an executive's strength is where the pastor is weakest. Rather than an occasion for friction or criticism, this is a golden opportunity for a business professional with a servant's heart to help strengthen the church.

One word of caution in this regard, however: many well-meaning professionals forget that their church is not a business enterprise. It does not function the way a secular organization does. Christ is the Head of the church. He provides its leadership. The church does not need power brokers or politicians. Administrators and business leaders are accustomed to being in charge, but in the church they are called upon to serve. The church needs people who hear from God and humbly obey him. Many times, people who spend all week in the corporate world bring the wrong attitude to their church. They pressure people to get what they want. They strong-arm their opinions in business meetings rather than seek a word from the church's Head. They guard the church finances against the "irresponsibility" of walking by faith. Their view is that when the surrounding community sees the church operating like a well-oiled machine, unbelievers will be attracted to the impressive product.

On the positive side, men and women from the corporate world have much to offer their church. Perhaps you should take your pastor out for lunch and ask him two things: 1) How could you use my skills and passions to serve the congregation? 2) How can I use my resources to encourage the pastoral staff and their families? Be prepared: the answer may involve you in ways you've never considered.

Watch for needs in your church that you or your company can meet. God placed you in your church for many reasons. It's an exciting venture to explore what those reasons are.

Questions for Reflection

1. How are you serving in your church? How has God confirmed that this is the area where he wants you right now?
2. Do you inadvertently operate in a worldly manner in your church? If so, what adjustments should you make?
3. Does the pastoral staff in your church see you as a blessing to them and to the congregation? Why or why not?
4. Has God been leading you to a ministry you have never considered before? If so, what are you doing in response?

Additional Resources

Henry Blackaby and Melvin Blackaby, *A God-Centered Church: Experiencing God Together* (Nashville: Broadman & Holman, 2007).

Kent Humphries, *Lasting Investments: A Pastor's Guide for Equipping Workplace Leaders to Leave a Spiritual Legacy* (Colorado Springs: NavPress, 2004).

Elton Trueblood, *The Company of the Committed: A Manual of Action for Every Christian* (San Francisco: Harper and Row, 1980).

Elton Trueblood, *The Incendiary Fellowship* (New York: Harper and Row, 1961; reprint ed. 1967).

How do I effectively encourage my pastor?

Paul said, "But now God has placed the parts, each one of them, in the body just as He wanted" (1 Cor. 12:18). According to 1 Corinthians 12, each Christian has a special, essential place in the local church. You are part of your congregation by the pleasure and purpose of God. You are not there as a spectator or as a critic. God wants to help your church experience him, and you have unique gifts and resources that may not be available to other members, including the pastoral staff.

It can be intimidating for a pastor to have a successful business leader in his congregation. When you see a weakness in your church or in your pastor, that is not an invitation to criticize but an opportunity to make a positive difference. Choose to support your pastor and to let him know you're behind him. Seek to meet with him and listen as he shares his heart. Pray with your pastor. Prayer unites people together.

We have both been pastors. We know that many hours of a pastor's day are taken up listening to people and caring for them. Yet the ministry can be a lonely calling in the sense that few church members know how to meet the personal needs of their minister. We know one CEO who has assumed the task of making sure his pastor takes a regular vacation as well as a weekly day off. Such practical concern can deeply impact your pastor's family. Seek to bless him by your words and actions, and even materially.

Most ministers are not highly paid, yet they are required to regularly extend hospitality to others. The drain on their energy and resources can be substantial.

Everyone has insecurities, and those in the ministry usually receive an abundance of critiques. God knows your pastor's weaknesses, just as he is aware of yours. You may be in a unique position to help your pastor, youth leader, or other ministers. As you concentrate on befriending your pastoral staff, God will reveal opportunities for you to help them and to bless their families. Strive to develop such a relationship with your church staff that every time they see you enter the church, they know they are greeting a friend.

Business leaders can find dozens of creative ways to bless their pastoral staff. Some buy them quality books or sponsor their attendance at first-class leadership seminars. Others offer their own cottages or condos to be used for much needed vacations or staff retreats. There are so many tangible ways to love ministers and their families: give them gifts, take them out to eat, bless their children. One couple regularly hosts Sunday lunch at their home. Their pastor and his family are always invited and are encouraged to invite a new or hurting family. In this way, the pastor's family is relieved of the effort and expense involved in hosting and is freed up to visit with the guests. Few church members realize how much their pastoral staff sacrifices for them. It is a tremendously rewarding experience to give something back. Find ways to bless your church staff. You might be surprised at what a difference it will make not only in their lives but in yours!

Questions for Reflection

1. How would you describe your relationship with your pastor? How would your minister describe it?
2. What have you done lately to affirm and encourage your church staff? What *could* you do?

3. What is your attitude toward your minister? Have you been critical? Do you need to extend forgiveness? Do you need to ask forgiveness?

4. What is a practical action you could take that would help your pastor's family? Make plans to do it soon.

Additional Resources

Romans 12:1–21
1 Corinthians 13:1–8
Ephesians 4:1–16
Colossians 4:6

Henry Blackaby and Melvin Blackaby, *A God-Centered Church: Experiencing God Together* (Nashville: Broadman & Holman, 2007).

Henry Blackaby and Melvin Blackaby, *What's So Spiritual About Your Gifts?* (Sisters, OR: Multnomah, 2004).

Richard Blackaby, *Putting a Face on Grace: Living a Life Worth Passing On* (Sisters, OR: Multnomah, 2006).

Elton Trueblood, *The Company of the Committed: A Manual for Action for Every Christian* (San Francisco: Harper and Row, 1980).

If my church is not functioning like it ought to, should I leave and find another one?

We have the privilege of speaking in conferences and churches all over North America and across the world. One of the most common, heart-breaking concerns people relate to us is that they know their church is functioning far below the level God intends for it.

After going through the studies *Experiencing God* or *Experiencing God Together,* many people have grown excited about what their church could do. But when they shared their enthusiasm with their church leader-ship, their ideas were dismissed. These disillusioned people want to know what they should do. They see that corporate prayer times are nonexistent in their congregation and that their church is failing to reach their neigh-borhood for Christ. They want to help infuse life and hope into the body, yet their church leaders view them as a threat to their authority rather than a spark plug for revival. Discouraged and disheartened, many have approached us and tearfully asked if they should leave their church to find one that is more active.

This is a difficult question. Often these people have been labeled by the church staff as troublemakers and have been excluded from church leadership. Some have been accused of dividing the church, or their efforts to bring change have been misjudged. They are seen as critics who think they have an inside track to God or are more spiritual than the rest of the church members. Their disenchantment is painful to observe. Many have been longtime church members and have faithfully served in numerous ministry positions. Yet continuing to bring their families to church means subjecting themselves and those they love to a dead congregation with life-less programs.

If you are in such a situation, here is some food for thought:

First, we would say again, Christ is the one who adds members to the body (1 Cor. 12:18). If he led you to your church, he will release you if you are to go elsewhere. Be sure you have a clear sense of God's leading *away* from your church. Do not merely leave because your church is undergoing problems.

A second and valid consideration is your family. You may worry that your children are being spiritually stifled at your current church. This issue is a critical one, so be sure you get *God's* perspective on your situation. He may want your family right where it is for the same reason you are consider-ing moving them—their spiritual growth. Be careful what you teach your children. We have known sincere Christians who moved their children to three or four churches over the course of five years. In their minds, these parents were seeking a church that would best minister to their family. What they were actually doing, however, was teaching their children to be fussy church hoppers. The message communicated was: if you don't like what your church is doing, leave.

These parents *could* have taught their children a different lesson. They could have modeled perseverance and loyalty. They could have asked God to use their family to make a difference. They could have been on their knees interceding for the people who were causing the most problems and asking the Father to intervene redemptively. They might have taught their family to act in a Christlike manner toward those who were behaving in an unchristian way. Perhaps if they and other families like them had stayed at their posts, they could have rejoiced one day that they had participated in God's activity to heal and restore his church. Powerful lessons learned in the midst of adversity could spark spiritual growth in your children and prepare them to be faithful church members as adults. We parents are protective, and we want the best for our children. We just need to make sure we are seeking God's best and not merely the easiest path.

Third, if the leadership of your church is not walking in the Spirit and is not shepherding the people as they ought, you may be more needed by your church right now than ever before. We have seen the scenario far too many times—a congregation calls a new minister who begins radically to change the spirit and focus of the church. Longtime, faithful members see where the new leadership is headed, and they begin to leave the church in droves. Weaker, vulnerable members are left with no one to care for them, and they suffer grievously. Then after a brief, tumultuous tenure, the pastor moves on, leaving a remnant of church members wounded and bewildered. Unfortunately, by then many of the stronger Christians who could have rallied the church and cared for the suffering members have already departed and are now actively serving in nearby churches.

Sometimes the very thing you grieve over in your church is the reason you should stay. If you have a heart for prayer but your pastor does not share your burden, it may be all the more necessary that you remain at your church. There will be those who need the encouragement of your prayers. If your church staff will not call people to pray, you may need to be the catalyst who mobilizes people to intercede for your church. If your pastor is only concerned about evangelism and has no time for homebound or elderly members, it may be that you should continue to minister to that group, lest they go neglected. Your church may seem uninterested in missions, but perhaps some in your congregation would gladly respond if you planned a mission trip or led a missions study.

We know one businessman who seriously considered leaving his church because it had no men's ministry and he felt the need for one. Rather than releasing him to go to another church, however, God led this man to begin a fledgling men's ministry in his own church. To his surprise, numerous men responded enthusiastically. With his motivational and organizational skills, this businessman experienced the joy of leading a thriving men's ministry that soon began to draw men from all over the city. He discovered that men in his community felt the same way he did. God had sensitized this man to a particular need so he could be a part of God's answer for that community.

If you are particularly sensitive to an aspect of church life that is not functioning as it should, that is not necessarily your cue to depart; it may be your reason for being there. God equips his people for whatever he calls them to do. If you have teenagers, for example, but the youth program is weak or nonexistent, ask God what he wants you and your teens to do. Don't say, "Oh, that's not my thing—*finance* is my area of giftedness." God may guide you to open your home to host youth events and to chaperone the next youth outing. Always keep in mind that God knew what your church would go through before he led you to join it. Perhaps this period of need in your church is the reason God wanted you in its membership.

Fourth, if you are disappointed in or frustrated with your pastor, remember that as a Christian, you have the ministry of reconciliation (2 Cor. 5:18). Jesus commanded us to love one another (John 15:17). A disciple with the mind and heart of Christ refuses to take offense at a fellow believer. Love always believes the best (1 Cor. 13:7). Disgruntlement is an attitude one adopts. Decide ahead of time that regardless of what others say or do, you will continue to be Christlike. This definitely takes God's empowerment, but he will make you "strong in the grace that is in Christ Jesus" (2 Tim. 2:1).

After prayerfully examining your own heart in regards to the previous four points, you may still conclude it is best for you to find a new church. God knows the future, and he may choose to remove you and your family from your present congregation. He may plan to use you to enrich another church that is seeking to follow his leading. If God does release you to leave, be sure to depart on the best possible terms. Refuse to say unkind words about the leadership or people. Don't sneak out the back door. Take opportunities to thank all those who touched your life while you were in their fellowship. Thank the pastor and church leaders for their efforts, even if you do not agree with all they have done. Refrain from taking parting shots at their leadership. You will never regret being gracious. Doing so may allow you the freedom to return and visit the church on occasion and to maintain friendships with its members. Regardless of how others behaved, there is no excuse for you to act in an unchristlike way in your interactions with the church.

Questions for Reflection

1. Are you experiencing frustration and disappointment with your church? If so, why?
2. As you have sought God, what has he told you your role in the body is to be during this difficult time?
3. Has your behavior toward fellow church members been Christlike? How might you better reflect Christ to people during this challenging period?

Additional Resources

Henry Blackaby and Melvin Blackaby, *A God-Centered Church: Experiencing God Together* (Nashville: Broadman & Holman, 2007).

Melvin Blackaby, *Going the Second Mile: Letting God Take You Beyond Yourself* (Sisters, OR: Multnomah, 2006).

Richard Blackaby, *Putting a Face on Grace: Living a Life Worth Passing On* (Sisters, OR: Multnomah, 2006).

Should I stay at my church if they won't utilize my gifts and experience?

It is commendable for you to want to make the maximum contribution in your congregation, knowing that churches can indeed be careless in using the skills and expertise of their members. But again, a church is not a business, so it will not necessarily function like one. While God definitely has plans for every member of the body to contribute, those plans may not look the way you might expect.

It is important to distinguish between your natural, tested abilities and your spiritual gifts. Natural aptitudes can be anything from musical talent to administrative or financial skills. They include things we do for a living and those for which we receive praise and recognition. Such abilities can be improved with experience and coaching. Capabilities such as intelligence or stamina can greatly complement a person's skills. Spiritual gifts, however, reflect the equipping of God's people by the Holy Spirit for divine assignments.

The Holy Spirit resides within every Christian. One of the Spirit's assignments is to empower believers so they can obey what God tells them to do. Therefore, if God places you in a church body and asks you to teach Sunday school in the children's department, the Holy Spirit will equip you to communicate biblical truth in a way little ones can understand. This divine equipping, however, is unnecessary if you do not follow the Spirit's leading and agree to teach youngsters. Biblically, God always empowered people *after* he gave them an assignment. There is a line of thinking that assumes people are given a "spiritual gift" at the time of their conversion, a gift that remains with them, unchanged for life, regardless of whether the person uses it or not. The testimony of the Bible, however, is that God first gives an assignment and then he equips people to accomplish it. This means God can change your assignments numerous times over the course of your walk with him, and he may lead you to serve him in ways you did not anticipate. The key is not your natural aptitude or even your training in a particular capacity but the Spirit's commitment to prepare you to do anything your heavenly Father assigns.

Business professionals can inadvertently rely strictly on their natural and learned expertise in serving their church rather than the Holy Spirit's gifting. They know their strengths; they have used them to achieve success in the business world. They naturally assume those same abilities can benefit their local church. So, for example, if a businesswoman is skilled in long-range planning, she may assume she should be on her church's long-range planning committee. Or an executive in the marketing industry may want to find ways to promote his church in the community. But if their churches do not seem to need or want their involvement in those areas, they may become frustrated and consider looking for another church. If this has happened to you, there are several things to consider.

Is this a matter of pride? The business world has its own way of recognizing, praising, and rewarding talent. You may be accustomed to accolades for your strong performance. You may be used to standing out among your peers as particularly successful. When you enter your church, however, you are on level ground with every other child of God. In fact, service is what is honored in God's kingdom, not superiority. You may receive deferential treatment in your company, and perhaps you expect the same at church.

Could it be that God is pruning you of pride by not highlighting your expertise in your church? Jesus adamantly declared, "You can do nothing without Me" (John 15:5). All your skills and talents will not affect eternity one bit. Only what Christ does through your life really matters. So invite the Holy Spirit to accomplish his divine work through your life. He may lead you to undertake a ministry you have never done before, or even one that lies outside your skill set. But when he works through you, lives will be changed.

Allow the Holy Spirit to direct where you serve in your church. You may gravitate toward the finance committee or the elder board, but the Spirit may lead you to join the hospital visitation ministry, to chaperone a youth mission trip, or to assist the prison ministry. Serving out of your usual area will highlight your dependence on the Spirit's strength and guidance. Doing so can also be a refreshing, exhilarating experience as you see God doing his work in ways you know only he can do.

Finally, realize that people can prevent you from serving on a committee or in a particular capacity, but no one can stop the Holy Spirit from using your life to bless others. The only person who can limit your usefulness is you. Your pride can render you ineffective in your church. James exhorts believers: "Humble yourselves before the Lord, and He will exalt you" (James 4:10). If you feel under-used, God may be prompting you to seek his direction or to help others serve God to their maximum. Serving in church is all about knowing God and edifying others. It is a place of great fulfillment and deep contentment; it is not an arena for self-promotion. If you understand the difference, you are ready for God to use you.

Questions for Reflection

1. How are you presently serving in your church? What is the evidence that God placed you in that position?
2. Why do you think God led you to your current position(s) of ministry? How do others benefit from what you are doing?

3. How would God evaluate the attitude you have shown in serving him through your church? How might your attitude be improved?
4. Are you preventing others from serving in a capacity to which God may be calling them? If so, how will you change?
5. Is there a need in your church that you feel God is directing you to address? What is holding you back?

Additional Resources

Matthew 16:18–19
Romans 12:3–21
1 Corinthians 12
Galatians 5:22–25; 6:1–6
Ephesians 4:11–12
Colossians 1:18

Henry Blackaby and Melvin Blackaby, *What's So Spiritual about Your Gifts?* (Sisters, OR: Multnomah, 2004).
Henry Blackaby and Melvin Blackaby, *A God-Centered Church: Experiencing God Together* (Nashville: Broadman & Holman, 2007).
Richard Blackaby, *Unlimiting God: Increasing Your Capacity to Experience the Divine* (Colorado Springs: Multnomah, 2008).

How should I become involved in my community?

The psalmist wrote: "How happy is the man who does not follow the advice of the wicked, or take the path of sinners, or join a group of mockers! Instead, his delight is in the LORD's instruction, and he meditates on it day and night. He is like a tree planted beside streams of water that bears its fruit in season and whose leaf does not wither. Whatever he does prospers" (Ps. 1:1–3).

Wouldn't it be great to have a neighbor like that?

Henry's father, Gerald Blackaby, was such a man. For many years, he was a manager for the Bank of Montreal in western Canada. He saw his *profession* as running a bank, but he understood his *calling* as a servant of God. When the bank transferred him to Prince Rupert, an isolated town in northern Canada, he realized God was moving his life and family to a place that desperately needed the gospel. For the next decade, he sought to be a channel of blessing in that community. He and his wife and three children started a church that continues to this day. He would often share his faith with clients who told him of their financial despair. As a result, he regularly saw people put their faith in Christ. He also volunteered in numerous capacities, seeking to make a positive difference in his community.

Eventually, when Gerald was transferred to another district, the local paper carried an article praising him for his Christian character and the

GOD IN THE MARKETPLACE

many contributions he had made to the town. He had been like a strong tree that bore much fruit in his season there. Forty-five years after Gerald Blackaby's death, Richard and his son Mike were visiting a church in the Middle East. After Richard spoke at the service, a couple approached them and said, "We became Christians in the church your grandfather started in Prince Rupert!" Sixty years later, that banker's descendents are still hearing people praise God for his faithfulness to God's calling on his life.

Ask yourself: "Why did God place me in this city? Why did I choose a house in this neighborhood? What did God know this area needed when he led me here?" We know scores of business people who are keenly sensitive to their calling to a particular locality. Some have become leaders in their community associations. Many use their company resources to bless their town or offer the services of their company for local causes. Some lend their facilities to local organizations. Others volunteer on local committees or sponsor community events. Many have made substantial donations to worthy causes.

Wherever you live, you can better your community and glorify God in doing so. Some business people we know host appreciation banquets for the local clergy. One Christian manager of a car dealership gives special rates to clergy. He also freely donates his time and energy into projects to improve his town. His town recognized him as its citizen of the year last year.

When the Israelites were carted off to bondage in Babylon, God instructed them through Jeremiah: seek the peace of the city in which you dwell, for in its peace, you will have peace (Jer. 29:7). The same creative genius and energy that characterize your career can bless those in your community. Ask God to direct your attention to how he wants to bless people through you.

Questions for Reflection

1. What positive contribution are you making to your community?
2. Why do you think God led you to your particular neighborhood?
3. Are there new ways God could use your life to bless your community?

Additional Resources

Proverbs 3:27; 10:7; 10:11, 10:31; 11:25; 14:34; 19:17; 22:1; 22:9; 25:6–7; 27:10; 27:21

Matthew 5:13–16; 9:8

Acts 4:13; 19:8–10

Philippians 2:15

1 Peter 2:11–12

Henry Blackaby, *Created to Be God's Friend: How God Shapes Those He Loves* (Nashville: Thomas Nelson, 1999).

Henry Blackaby and Norman Blackaby, *Called and Accountable: Discovering Your Place in God's Eternal Purpose*, revised ed., (Birmingham, AL: New Hope Publishers, 2005).

Richard Blackaby, *Unlimiting God: Increasing Your Capacity to Experience the Divine* (Colorado Springs: Multnomah, 2008).

J. B. Phillips, *Your God Is Too Small* (New York: The Macmillan Company, 1961; reprint ed., 1971).

Wes Cantrell
Former Chairman and Chief Executive Officer
Lanier Worldwide

I had been with Lanier just a few years, but I knew what I wanted. The district managers' position appeared to be the most desirable job in the company, and I believed my major strengths were in management, not in being a salesman for the rest of my life. I was about to find out if I was right.

In 1961, Gene Milner called and asked me to come to Atlanta to discuss the future of the company. In the process, he offered me the job as district manager of Baton Rouge. This was the most exciting news I could have imagined. It was the job I wanted, and it was also in an ideal location since it was my wife's home. In addition, I had been there in my first assignment, and I knew the territory and many of the people.

Little did I know how difficult the transition from selling to management could be. I had heard of many great salesmen who failed in management assignments. I understood that managing involved the use of a different set of skills and that many were unable to make the transition. Couple that with youth—I was only 26 years old—and lack of exposure, and you can understand the degree of difficulty. I had no management training and had only worked in small offices with just a few employees. I was really green behind the ears!

In my previous job, I had only been responsible for selling our products in Augusta, Georgia. Now I had to recruit new sales and service reps. The management and motivation of people was all new to me. I had never conducted a sales meeting. I had never seen a profit and loss statement, which was now the basis of my compensation. I had lots of new skills to learn, and I didn't have much time.

There was one other tough issue. A salesman in Baton Rouge, who was number one in company standings, was sure that he should have been appointed manager. And he plotted against me from the beginning, ridiculing me behind my back.

I was very naïve and trusting. I had never had to handle any situation like this before. I had great difficulty in thinking that I should fire the number one salesman in the company. But I knew that he was a negative influence on the new and highly talented people I was bringing into the company.

To make matters even worse, I had a boss whose value system was almost exactly opposite of mine. Everything I held dear in life was not important to him and vice versa. Although we got along on the surface, we were not in harmony, and this put additional pressure on me. Yet he was the person assigned to teach me how to manage!

Within a few months, it was obvious I was failing as a manager. We had difficulty selling our home in Augusta, which brought even more pressure. It seemed as though everything that could go wrong did! I was very discouraged. This was the only time in my forty-six years with Lanier that I interviewed for another job.

But there was light at the end of the tunnel. I had hired some very good sales reps, and some of them were doing quite well. But there was something wrong in the organization. I could sense it, and I knew it was holding us back.

It was during this time that some of the new reps confided in me that the disloyal sales rep was having meetings, poking fun at what I said and did. He was doing everything in his power to see that I failed while he continued to sell extremely well.

I confronted him about this and he promised he would stop. He even shed tears of repentance and promised to work to help me build a great team. But in a few short days, I learned that he had continued to undermine my leadership.

Shortly after this, while away at a management development meeting, I made the decision to fire him. It wasn't an easy or snap decision, but I knew it was in the company's best interest.

I decided that the right time to do it was the Monday he was set to return from a trip to New York, having been one of the winners of our annual incentive trip. He came back bragging and showing off his awards. I called him into my office and told him to pack up his things, as he was no longer employed there. He was totally shocked because he thought it would never happen. He stomped out of the office in a huff.

Immediately, however, a breath of fresh air flowed throughout the office. We reassigned all territories and everyone was very excited. Business started to improve right away. It seemed easy for the production of the disloyal rep to be replaced by the increased production of all other reps. And that's exactly what happened.

In just a few days, I received a call from Gene Milner. I was somewhat unnerved, thinking he would jump all over me for firing the top rep in the company. But that's not what happened at all. He said, "I've always known you had to fire that guy, but you had to decide for yourself. It was a part of your growing up process. Today, you became a man, my boy."

I was greatly relieved and very excited to receive this call. It was confirmation of a difficult decision and it came at just the right time.

However, this development only set the stage for another major decision that was to determine the spiritual direction for the rest of my life. Although the district was performing better, it was still not what it should be, and I knew that very well. The Lord had a special message for me, and he wanted to be sure I listened. Failure is a marvelous platform for listening and learning. I was ready!

Returning to Baton Rouge after a short business trip, my wife suggested we go to hear an evangelist who was speaking at our church that night. I agreed to go, even though I was very tired.

But during the service that night, the Lord revealed several important truths to me. I realized that God had a will and purpose for all areas of my life, not just family and church, but I had never included the Lord in my business. It was in a separate compartment. I never consulted him about it or thought he even cared. But my thinking was all wrong about business as it relates to the Christian life.

That night was the beginning of a totally new spiritual journey for me. Immediately, I began to pray about all business decisions and ask the Lord for his blessing. I prayed much about the people I was hiring and that the Lord would send just the right people to build the team there in the Baton Rouge district. And he did!

You could draw a line—before and after this experience—and the "after" results in the district were simply fabulous. In four years, we went from $400,000 annual sales to more than $1.7 million.

These results were the stepping stones to my next promotion, moving back to Atlanta in 1966 to become general manager for all dictation operations. I was definitely on the move, and the Lord was defintely driving it. I could only dream of what he had in mind for the future, but I knew I was in his hand.

Wes Cantrell started with Lanier as a technician in 1955 and stayed with the same company for forty-six years, ending his career as chairman and CEO. He graduated from Southern Polytechnic State University and was recently honored with doctorate, the first ever granted to an alumnus. Wes, coauthor of the book *High Performance Ethics*, became a member of the Horatio Alger Association in 2001. He lives in Atlanta with his wife, Bernadine. They have four children, twenty-two grandchildren, and one great-grandchild, and are members of First Baptist Church, Woodstock.

PART 6

My Kingdom Life

God's kingdom, his total rule in the world, includes every local church over which Christ is Head as well as every believer (John 3:3, 5). Christ spoke far more about the kingdom of God than he did about the church. Jesus' first sermon, in fact, was on repentance and the kingdom of God (Mark 1:15). He sent his disciples out in pairs to preach about God's kingdom (Luke 9:2). God's kingdom was always a dominant concern for the Lord Jesus, so it ought to be prominent in our thoughts, priorities, and actions, as well.

Jesus promised that if we are faithful in a little, God will give us responsibility for much (Matt. 25:21; Luke 19:17). As many Christian businesspeople have grasped this promise, we have seen God honor their commitment and entrust them with increasing kingdom responsibility. We know several Christian leaders who have been promoted from regional directors to national CEOs and ultimately to positions overseeing their company's global operations. God has honored their devotion to him and has placed them next to world leaders, opening up opportunities for them to impact entire nations for Christ. So don't focus merely on the activities and responsibilities that are immediately before you. Always keep in mind that God views your life from a global, eternal perspective. God knows how to maximize your life for the greatest good for his kingdom. As a Christian, you are a kingdom citizen, and God ultimately has plans for you which exceed anything you could imagine (Matt. 28:18–20; Eph. 3:20).

How does my business fit into God's kingdom?

God continually exercises his sovereignty across the world. Wherever you are, you can find God accomplishing his purposes. As a kingdom citizen, you have the capacity to recognize God's activity throughout his realm (Matt. 13:11, 16). Christians enjoy the privilege of participating in God's plans. But the extent to which God invites you to join in his kingdom work depends on your heart's condition (Mark 6:52; 8:17–18). Your willingness to serve God is reflected in your obedience and faithfulness to him (John 14:21, 23; 15:14).

We see God working powerfully to mobilize his people, placing them in strategic settings around the globe. Like Joseph and Daniel of the Old Testament, more and more Christian businesspeople are recognizing that their positions of influence provide inroads to advance God's kingdom in ways inaccessible to pastors and missionaries. Some corporate leaders have access to nations that are closed to religious organizations. Even governments that are hostile to Christians are generally eager for business and technology from North America. Commerce opens doors into most countries. We know international executives who give Bibles and Christian materials to world leaders. Many business leaders donate company products to aid poverty-stricken countries and to provide a platform for sharing the gospel.

One executive offered a valuable product to impoverished villages in a Muslim country. His one stipulation was that he be free to tell people his motivation for doing so: his faith in Jesus Christ. In the first village, the majority of the population became Christians through his efforts. The Muslim national government leader was so impressed by this CEO's generosity, he asked him to do the same for a hundred similar villages.

The exciting thing about kingdom work is that there is no mandatory retirement. Many retired businesspeople use their flexible schedules to benefit God's kingdom. One man started a new company in his retirement for the sole purpose of investing the profits into Christian work, and God is blessing his business. Several retired business leaders we know are excited about new avenues God is opening up for them to serve him. Some are meeting with businesspeople in major world cities and teaching them how to be spiritual leaders in the marketplace. Several of these cities are in locations that are closed to missionaries. Christian businesspeople voluntarily teach business practices in other countries so these national business leaders can hear the gospel. Efforts are being made to place business leaders from North America alongside Christian government leaders of Third World countries. These governments desperately want to turn their national economies around, to create jobs, to alleviate the suffering of the poor, and to build infrastructure throughout their country. Some of these nations have guerilla organizations seeking to topple their government. What a magnificent opportunity, then, for experienced businesspeople to help Christian government leaders as they seek to reform their nations. The retired executives we work with are much more challenged and invigorated by these opportunities than by merely knocking a few strokes off their golf game at the country club.

Whether you are just starting out in your career or are retired, numerous exciting opportunities await you as a kingdom citizen. God always seeks to do far more in the world around us than our limited vision comprehends. We tend to develop a myopic view of our lives while God operates in the context of his entire dominion. Ask God to open your eyes to the ways he wants to use your life to impact the world.

Questions for Reflection

1. How is your life presently participating in God's work to extend his kingdom?
2. If God seems to be limiting your kingdom responsibility, what might the reason be?
3. How might you reorder your life so you are seeking God's kingdom *first* and trusting him to add everything else? (Matt. 6:33).

Additional Resources

Psalm 1:1–3
Proverbs 22:29
Zechariah 8:23
Malachi 3:10
Acts 1:8
Ephesians 3:20

Lloyd Reeb, *From Success to Significance: When the Pursuit of Success Isn't Enough* (Grand Rapids, MI: Zondervan, 2004).
Avery Willis, Jr. and Henry T. Blackaby, *On Mission with God: Living God's Purpose for His Glory* (Nashville: Broadman & Holman, 2002).

How should I use my position financially for the kingdom of God?

Jesus cautioned that it is foolish to invest all of your time and energy pursuing riches. Even a vast fortune is inconsequential once you reach your life's end (Luke 12:16–21). Jesus urged his followers to store their wealth in heaven rather than accumulate temporal, material wealth on earth (Luke 17:33; 18:28–30).

The tax collector Zacchaeus bought entirely into worldly values (Luke 19:1–10). He chased wealth ruthlessly, wanting money so much that he betrayed his own countrymen to get it. No wonder he was a social outcast! Zacchaeus was willing to forfeit his self-respect, his friends, even his soul to accumulate riches. Then he met Jesus and instantly gained a radically new perspective on life. His possessions suddenly seemed worthless. Now he only cared to live for Jesus. He began to show generosity toward others that went far beyond the norm of his day (Luke 19:8). He felt free to give his wealth away now that he was devoted to God rather than to his money.

Fundamental to the Christian life is this principle: "The one who did not know and did things deserving of blows will be beaten lightly. Much will be required of everyone who has been given much. And even more will be expected of the one who has been entrusted with more" (Luke 12:48).

You are a manager of everything God places in your hands. If God favors you with a good education, a successful career, a comfortable income, a nice home, or other blessings, he will hold you accountable for how you use them. If you merely accumulate God's blessings for yourself and do not reinvest them into kingdom enterprises, he may remove what you already have (Matt. 25:24–30).

God expects our lives to reflect gratitude for all he has done for us. He wants us to channel his generosity to those around us (Matt. 18:21–35). Stingy people clearly do not fully appreciate what God has done for them.

Another biblical truth is: your heart will follow your money. Jesus declared, "For where your treasure is, there your heart will be also" (Luke 12:34). This verse is often interpreted to mean that your money will go where your allegiance is, that where you spend your money indicates what you hold dearest. While that may be so, the statement actually says the opposite. It claims your devotion will follow your money! If you have ever purchased stock, you undoubtedly started watching that stock more closely than you had before. Why? Because that was where your money was. If all your resources are directed toward feathering your own nest, your heart will focus on personal wealth. But if you give generously to a homeless shelter, a safe house for abused women, or a Bible college, you will soon find yourself absorbed in what God is doing through the ministry you have endowed.

We work with hundreds of Christian businesspeople who are generous philanthropists. Much of the work occurring in Christian ministries, in theological education and in mission causes today is made possible by these altruistic men and women who invest their wealth in God's work. We could tell numerous stories of how God motivated someone to contribute to a Christian cause and how that donation enabled a ministry to continue its efforts.

Richard was president of the Canadian Southern Baptist Seminary for thirteen years. Today he is its chancellor. Each year, the seminary administration sought to proceed with every ministry God initiated. This was always a challenge, and despite frugal spending, the seminary would inevitably run short of funds. Richard, his staff, and the students would pray, and inevitably someone whom the Lord impressed would make a donation. Every year, the generosity of godly patrons enabled the school to meet its financial obligations, and it continues to do so. How exhilarating it is to pray fervently for the Lord's provision and then to hear from someone whom God has led to provide the answer to those prayers! Likewise, how exciting to be the channel through whom God blesses one of his kingdom's ministries.

Jesus said: "No one can be a slave of two masters, since either he will hate one and love the other, or be devoted to one and despise the other. You cannot be slaves of God and of money" (Matt. 6:24). Clearly, one cannot give absolute loyalty to two masters. If money is your idol, then God must take second place, a position he is unwilling to occupy. Materialism can gradually get a vise grip on you without your awareness of its power over you. You can become addicted to wealth, just as people get addicted to alcohol or pornography. One way to determine whether or not your money is your god is to give it away. That is one of the intrinsic benefits of tithing (Mal. 3:8–10). Tithing is a regular practice of giving to the Lord a significant portion of your earnings, something that's difficult to do if the accumulation of money is your life pursuit. If you habitually tithe on your income, however, you are regularly affirming to yourself and to God that money does not control you—you control *it!*

Christians ought to be the most generous of all people. After all, we have received the most. How does one put a value on being adopted as God's child? (Rom. 8:16–17). How could you measure the worth of having all your sins forgiven? The question is: what does your level of generosity reveal about your gratitude for all God has done for you?

Questions for Reflection

1. Could you acknowledge that God owns your money and possessions? If so, what is the evidence?
2. Is it difficult for you to give to the Lord's causes? To what ministries do you presently contribute?
3. Have you sought the Lord's direction for specific ways to support his kingdom work?

Additional Resources

Proverbs 11:25
Matthew 18:21-35
Luke 12:34; 12:48; 14:26–33; 16:10; 16:19–31
James 2:5
1 Timothy 6:17–18
Revelation 3:17–18

Randy Alcorn, *The Treasure Principle: Discovering the Secret of Joyful Giving* (Sisters: OR: Multnomah, 2001).

Richard Blackaby, *Putting a Face on Grace: Living a Life Worth Passing On* (Sisters, OR: Multnomah, 2006).

Ken Blanchard and Truett Cathy, *The Generosity Factor: Discovering the Joy of Giving Your Time, Talent, and Treasure* (Grand Rapids, MI: Zondervan, 2002).

Ron Blue, *Generous Living: Finding Contentment through Giving* (Grand Rapids, MI: Zondervan, 1997).

Alan Gotthardt, *The Eternity Portfolio: A Practical Guide to Investing Your Money for Ultimate Results* (Wheaton, IL: Tyndale House, 2003).

How do I develop a godly, global vision for my life's mission?

Do you have a clear sense of meaning and direction for your life, or are you merely living by the default motivations everyone else follows? There is no greater way to invest your days than to participate in kingdom activity.

God is on mission to redeem fallen humanity from its sin and destruction. His purpose from the beginning of creation has been to transform people into the image of his beloved Son (Rom. 8:29–30). God was willing to expend an infinite price to ransom us from our sin (John 3:16; Rom. 5:8). As he looks upon the billions of people populating the earth, God knows every individual by name; he fashioned each one of us (Ps. 139:14–16). God understands the potential of every life. But like no one else, he also recognizes the full tragedy of an eternity apart from him (Matt. 8:12; Rom. 6:23; Rev. 20:11–15). Therefore, the Father ardently pursues a love relationship with us so we can have our sins forgiven and enjoy eternity with him.

To this end, God is marshalling his servants to accomplish his purposes all over the world. His people are boldly sharing their faith in every country on the globe, including nations where Christianity is illegal. Thousands of believers risk their lives every day for the cause of Christ. God's people are traveling at their own expense on mission trips to testify to their faith. There are currently more ways to share Jesus with people than at any time in history. People sit at their computers and witness to those in countries officially closed to the gospel. Disaster relief teams are entering remote regions of the world and expressing God's love to victims of catastrophe.

You may not have grown up in a church or denomination that emphasized missions. Perhaps you've felt that people should take care of those in their own country before extending their resources abroad. After all, there are plenty of needy people in America, right? International missions may not often cross your mind. If this is the case, could we challenge you to investigate the possibility that God may have plans for you on a global level?

First, seek to learn about other countries and their spiritual condition. Both of us have lived in Canada for much of our lives. Canada and the U.S. share the longest undefended border in the world, and yet many Americans assume (incorrectly) that the level of Christian faith in Canada matches that in the U.S. In fact, the percentage of Christians in Canada is significantly lower.

There are many ways to become educated about the spiritual needs in other countries. Read books and magazines about missions and world religions. Adopt a missionary family and correspond with them. Seek to encourage them through prayer and care packages. Make the effort to travel to see other cultures firsthand.

We have helped our children see the world. Richard's children have grown up in a predominantly white, middle-class, suburban environment. So Richard and Lisa have deliberately sought to expose them to mission activity. Their middle son, Daniel, following high school graduation, spent a year doing international mission work. He went to South Africa, Botswana, Greece, Brazil, Norway, and Germany. He came home with the world on his heart. Richard's oldest son, Mike, has done mission work in South Africa, Botswana, Greece, the Bahamas, Singapore, Malaysia, and a Middle Eastern country. Richard's daughter Carrie has accompanied her dad on speaking trips to England, Norway, Germany, Singapore, Malaysia, Australia, and New Zealand. She has witnessed God's work in each of these countries. Why is this important? Because we live in a global village, and we must have the world on our hearts as God does.

Second, ask God to show you how your life can impact the world for Christ. We know people who have been Christians most of their lives and yet have never been on a mission trip. Too often, Christians assume that their mission commitment is fulfilled merely by dropping money into the offering plate at church. Christians have a much greater obligation than that.

As Jesus prepared to leave his disciples and ascend to his Father, he gave them one final command: "But you will receive power when the Holy Spirit has come upon you, and you will be My witnesses in Jerusalem, in all Judea and Samaria, and to the ends of the earth" (Acts 1:8). Jesus had completed his assignment. He had died for humanity's sins and been resurrected so those who repented of their sin and trusted in him could experience eternal life. The task at hand was to tell people about the divine gift available to them. So Christ commanded his disciples to look beyond themselves to their neighborhood, their community, their nation, and the entire world. Jesus did *not* say, "Those of you with the gift of evangelism," or, "Those of you who feel called to international missions." *Every* disciple is responsible to be a witness to him locally and globally.

Unfortunately, when many Christians read this command, they immediately reinterpret it as saying, "You will be my witnesses where you live, and you will pray for people in other places and give money to missions so others can be witnesses in regions where you cannot go." Is that what Christ meant? No, he commanded each of his disciples to take the good news to the entire earth.

Never minimize a command from Jesus. Ask him what this directive looks like for you. Does this mean you quit your job and roam from country to country handing out gospel tracts until you run out of money? Probably not. Does it mean God intends for you to nurture a passion to see the world come to Christ? Absolutely.

What will your participation in God's mission to redeem humanity look like? Certainly it will include intercessory prayer. You cannot claim to have the unredeemed of the world on your heart and never pray for them. Stay informed about God's activity around the world. Consider participating in mission trips nationally and internationally. Check with your church and denomination for mission opportunities. Is there a region of the world toward which God has sensitized you? If God lays a geographical area on your heart, recognize it as God's activity, and look for ways he wants you to become involved in carrying the name of Christ to that place.

We could tell numerous stories of professional people who responded to God as he gave them a burden for a particular country or race. We know an American businesswoman who built an orphanage in Asia. We know a businessman from California who is combating AIDS in Africa. We know a pathologist in Texas who passionately supports the training of ministers in Canada. We know a farmer from Illinois who led a church-planting effort in Brazil. We know a Canadian engineer who began a church in a Muslim country. These are not missionaries by trade; they are ordinary people with a heart for missions. And examples like these are endless. Whenever God gets his people's attention and lays his heart over theirs, the world feels the impact.

Finally, if you are involved in international business travel, recognize that God has a purpose for your job that surpasses merely opening foreign markets for your company. We know an American businessman who gives a Bible to government leaders of foreign countries. We know a lay couple who gave a copy of *Experiencing God* to the ruler of a militant Muslim country. Numerous professionals who regularly travel internationally have identified local churches in the areas they visit, and they make a point to worship with those believers and to encourage them.

When Henry was a pastor in Saskatoon, Canada, a man named Bob from Colorado contacted him. Bob was going to be conducting research at the University in Saskatoon for several months, and he wanted to know how he could help Henry's church. While Bob and his family were in Canada, they began a boys' club in the church. He and his wife also launched the first annual provincial summer youth camp for the denomination. The church felt the impact of Bob's visit for years to come. Bob and his wife returned several times afterward, and each time they blessed the church. Bob took the opportunity while working internationally to invest his life in God's kingdom. A number of young men in that boys' club grew up with a heart for missions, and several have served as missionaries and pastors. Richard was one of them.

God's heart is for people. He is not willing that anyone should perish (John 3:16). So if you are going to have a heart like God's, you must think globally—as he does—and invest your life in missions. Your life has the opportunity to impact the world. Why would you settle for anything less?

Questions for Reflection

1. What are some ways God is using your life to spread his kingdom around the world?
2. What region of the world has God placed on your heart? What part of the world have you always wanted to visit? What might you do to become more involved in reaching that place for Christ?
3. Have you ever been on a mission trip? What would you need to do to go on one this year?
4. What countries do you interact with through your profession? How might you invest in God's kingdom through your business travel and contacts?
5. What percentage of your income do you invest in world evangelization? Could you give more?

Additional Resources

Andrew Murray, *Reaching Your World for Christ* (New Kensington, PA: Whitaker House, 1997).

John Piper, *Let the Nations Be Glad: The Supremacy of God in Missions* (Grand Rapids, MI: Baker Book House, 1993).

Avery Willis Jr., and Henry T. Blackaby, *On Mission with God: Living God's Purpose for His Glory* (Nashville: Broadman & Holman, 2002).

How involved should I be in politics?

The Bible says much about government. Scripture contends that God is the author of governments and that Christians are obligated to be good citizens (Rom. 13:1–7). Jesus taught that people ought to pay taxes (Matt. 22:15–22). Scripture further admonishes believers to pray for those in positions of governmental authority: "First of all, then, I urge that petitions, prayers, intercessions, and thanksgivings be made for everyone, for kings and all those who are in authority, so that we may lead a tranquil and quiet life in all godliness and dignity" (1 Tim. 2:1–2).

Praying for government leaders, then, is not an option; it is God's bidding. Regardless of whether your political party is currently in power or the national leader is the one who got your vote, you need to pray for your nation's leaders. God's people will get the government they pray for.

Henry recently had the opportunity to be the honorary chairman of the American National Day of Prayer. We were both at the White House the day when Henry delivered the primary address. Then we heard from the President. He emphasized that nothing we could do for him was more meaningful or important than to pray. In a time filled with so many complexities and dangers, how could we not pray regularly for our government's leaders?

It is propitious that Christians be informed, responsible citizens. This means taking time to understand the positions candidates hold and voting your conscience. Christians should not automatically vote for the same party every election without investigating the individuals who are running for office. Our desire ought not to be that our party wins the election but that the government is led by capable, godly public servants.

Scripture counsels believers to practice submission to authority and to live peaceably and honorably with all people (Rom. 12:18; Col. 3:18–23; Titus 3:1). Some Christians view all governments as enemies. Scripture, however, says the government serves a legitimate, God-ordained purpose.

When the Israelites were taken captive by the conquering Babylonians, they wondered how to respond to the idolatrous, pagan, hostile government of Babylon. This regime had destroyed Jerusalem and the holy temple. Here was God's reply:

> Build houses and live in them. Plant gardens and eat their produce. Take wives and have sons and daughters. Take wives for your sons and give your daughters to men in marriage so that they may bear sons and daughters. Multiply there; do not decrease. See the welfare of the city I have deported you to. Pray to the LORD on its behalf, for when it has prosperity, you will prosper. (Jer. 29:5–7)

God does not expect you to accept and support every government initiative, because some are ungodly and violate his Word. But he does expect his people to bless whatever nation they inhabit. In their heathen surroundings, believers are to be salt and light, sharing God's goodness wherever they live (Matt. 5:13–16).

The CEO group with whom we work has twice been invited to participate in White House briefings, hearing specific concerns and issues the government is facing. Every government needs trustworthy men and women who serve on various committees and task forces as well as in government roles. While we must not place our hope in governments (Ps. 20:7), we ought to do everything in our power to be a blessing to our nation.

Ultimately, however, believers must understand that our citizenship is not in an earthly nation but in heaven (Phil. 3:20). Christ has preeminence over every nation and administration (Ps. 2:4; Col. 1:16–18; Rev. 21:24). If you must choose between pleasing your government or the Lord, your loyalty should always be to God (Acts 4:17–20; 5:29). The history of the early church is peppered with accounts of Christians who chose to die rather than to deny their Lord. When the Roman officials sought to force believers to declare, "Caesar is Lord," brave Christians boldly replied, "*Jesus* is Lord." Untold thousands lost their lives because they would not obey their government if it meant dishonoring their Lord.

God has led numerous believers to become involved in politics. Several elected public servants have told us that after they studied *Experiencing God*, the Lord guided them to run for office. Christians are not to run from the world but to be transformational agents *in* the world (John 17:14–18). Those seeking political office must carefully examine their motives. Power is seductive, and pressure to conform is intense. Yet God has used government leaders to dramatically impact nations for good. Those who allow God to use them in the political realm can have enormous kingdom influence. One state senator filled a theater with government officials to see the movie *The Passion of the Christ*. An American senator recently led an *Experiencing God* study in the U.S. Senate. A group of state senators is presently meeting each week to study our book *Spiritual Leadership*. Several government leaders host weekly prayer meetings and Bible studies for their colleagues. Just as God elevated Joseph, Daniel, and Esther to high government posts in biblical times, so God seeks people who will faithfully serve him in government today.

Government leaders face pressures and difficult situations as never before. During our time at the White House, we were moved by how many congressmen, senators, and government and military officials pleaded with us to pray for them and their families. Christians in the government and military are under severe stress. We *must* uphold them in prayer. Our calling as believers is not to be critics but to make a difference for good. The world has plenty of armchair analysts but far too few prayer warriors.

Questions for Reflection

1. Are you a responsible, conscientious, informed citizen? What is the evidence of that?
2. Do you faithfully pray for your government leaders?
3. Have you placed too much faith and hope in government? If so, how have you done that?
4. Is there some level of involvement God wants you to have as an elected official of a school board, local organization, or government office?
5. What are some ways you could tangibly support your government leaders?

Additional Resources

Exodus 22:28
Acts 23:1–5
Proverbs 11:25
Acts 24:16
Titus 3:1

Mike Huckabee, *Character Makes a Difference* (Nashville: Broadman & Holman, 2007).

Eric Metaxes, *Amazing Grace: William Wilberforce and the Heroic Campaign to End Slavery* (New York: HarperSanFrancisco, 2007).

How involved should I become in social issues?

Two important life themes weave throughout Scripture: the physical and the spiritual. Clearly, God's primary concern is spiritual (Rom. 8:12–17). God is spirit (John 4:24), and only the spiritual world is eternal. God's main agenda concerns people's salvation, for that is what affects their eternity (John 11:25–26).

God also cares about people's physical needs, however. Scripture is filled with expressions of concern for the plight of suffering people. While God knows that our trials in this life are temporary, he expects believers to help others in need and to alleviate people's distress.

Throughout Scripture, God continually calls for people to take care of the less fortunate, including widows, orphans, and foreigners (Exod. 22:22–23; Deut. 10:18–19; Ps. 68:5; 146:9; Isa. 1:17, 23; Hos. 14:3; Zech. 7:10). Those whom society often overlooks are never out of God's sight.

God is also deeply concerned about injustice (Amos 4:1; 5:24; Mic. 6:8; Mal. 3:5). Justice is not just an Old Testament theme. Jesus was moved with compassion when he saw people in need and those being oppressed who had no advocate (Matt. 9:36). He declared that whenever one of his disciples cared for someone who lacked food, clothing, or shelter or who was in prison, they were ministering to him (Matt. 25:31–46). When John the Baptist was looking for confirmation that Jesus was the Messiah,

Jesus pointed to his ministry to the needy (Matt. 11:4–6). Jesus told the rich young ruler that if he wanted to be Jesus' disciple, he must sell his possessions and give them to the poor (Luke 18:22). Jesus' example of a true neighbor was the good Samaritan who took time to help a suffering foreigner (Luke 10:25–37). When Zacchaeus became Jesus' follower, he immediately gave half his wealth to the poor (Luke 19:8). Jesus clearly believed that true followers of God would not look the other way when they saw someone needing help.

The early church recognized that one of its fundamental responsibilities was to care for widows and orphans (Acts 6:1–7). The apostle James described a Christian's duty this way: "Pure and undefiled religion before our God and Father is this: to look after orphans and widows in their distress and to keep oneself unstained by the world" (James 1:27).

To honor God, one must share God's concerns. We tend to isolate ourselves from those who are destitute. We buy homes in safe, affluent neighborhoods or gated communities where we never see a homeless or hungry person. We consciously avoid areas of the city where we might encounter the down and out. Yet Jesus was drawn to poor, hungry, and sick people. In fact, Jesus said he would expose false believers by judging them for their behavior toward the hungry and needy (Matt. 25:31–46).

What can you do?

You can become informed. Go downtown and visit a Christian organization that ministers to the homeless and hungry. Serve in a soup line one day. Volunteer at a drug rehabilitation center. Find out what Christian ministries are doing to help people in the slums. Perhaps you could help teach refugees who are learning English or obtaining their high school diploma.

You can give. Numerous businesspeople generously support ministries to the poor. Most Christian organizations are run on shoestring budgets, and their operators are deeply appreciative of every donation. We know Christian couples who choose to live at a level below their income so they can direct more funds toward meeting the needs of those who have little.

Consider using your company resources to alleviate the suffering of others. Restaurant owners provide free meals to the poor. Bakeries deliver goods to homeless shelters. One businessman donated power plants to Third World villages in Africa. Another established a foundation to address pressing needs in Africa. A building contractor takes teams to South America to construct orphanages. We know many Christians who have unofficially adopted single moms; they assist them financially and in practical ways throughout the year, including covering the education costs of their children. The possibilities for helping others are endless. Don't be satisfied simply to pay your taxes, drop a twenty into the benevolent offering at church, and assume you have met your obligation to the poor. Ask the Lord what specific things you and your family should do to bring comfort to those who need it.

Questions for Reflection

1. What are you presently doing to address the needs of the poor, the homeless, widows, single parents, orphans, addicts, abused people, and foreigners?
2. What do you sense God wants you to do specifically to minister to the needy?
3. What adjustments, personal or financial, are necessary for you to more effectively help those in need?

Additional Resources

Exodus 23:6–9
Deuteronomy 24:17–22
Proverbs 23:10–11
Isaiah 61:1, 8
Ezekiel 34

Amos 5:24
Habakkuk 1:2–4
John 12:8
Galatians 2:10
James 2:5

Randy Alcorn, *The Treasure Principle: Discovering the Secret of Joyful Giving* (Sisters, OR: Multnomah, 2001).

Ron Blue, *Generous Living: Finding Contentment through Giving* (Grand Rapids, MI: Zondervan, 1997).

Eric Metaxes, *Amazing Grace: William Wilberforce and the Heroic Campaign to End Slavery* (New York: HarperSanFrancisco, 2007).

Lloyd Reeb, *From Success to Significance: When the Pursuit of Success Isn't Enough* (Grand Rapids, MI: Zondervan, 2004).

CONCLUSION

The four weathered fishermen began their day as they always did. But this day would be extraordinary. As the men repaired their nets and performed the mundane tasks of their trade, they suddenly realized they were not alone. Jesus was standing beside their boat. "Follow me," he said, "and I will make you fishers of men." There was no detailed explanation. There was no long-range plan. There were no promises of perks and prosperity. There was just a singularly clear, direct, and life-changing invitation. They could remain where they were and experience a relatively secure, comfortable, predictable life. Or they could lay aside their routine, their previous plans and goals, and go with the teacher.

The world has felt the impact for the last two thousand years of the decision those fishermen made.

God is powerfully at work in our world today. Numerous indications reveal we are living in the final days before Jesus' return. The threat of global terrorism makes a worldwide holocaust a frightening possibility. The swelling numbers of people populating the earth who have never heard the gospel and who do not follow Jesus as their Lord make clear that the church cannot continue merely doing business as usual. These are critical days, and God is marshalling his people to accomplish a divine work of unprecedented proportions.

In our generation, Jesus is calling more than fishermen and tax collectors to walk with him. The Lord is entering corporate offices and inviting businesspeople to join him. He is calling professionals from every field and mobilizing them for his kingdom agenda. God is adjusting the goal-setting and career plans of businesspeople around the world. Men and women in the business world are discovering the joy of accomplishing far more than earning money and climbing the corporate ladder. They are finding themselves in the midst of God's mighty work in the marketplace, and as a result they are experiencing the most fulfilling and rewarding days in their lives.

Now is the time to join God in his exciting work. The possibilities for serving God today are limitless. Technology allows us to impact our world in ways undreamed of a generation ago. God is moving forward to accomplish his cosmic purposes. Are you prepared to join him? Are you willing to live in such a way that you impact not only your world but eternity?

It is exciting to meet businesspeople from around the world who are determined to make extending God's kingdom their highest priority. You may be one of the many people who are adjusting their priorities and schedules to be a part of God's activity. If so, you will see your walk with God reach new levels of intimacy and power that you never dreamed possible.

Our hope is that you will continue to grow in your walk with God and in your service for him. Take time to reflect on what God taught you as you studied this book. In light of all he has shown you, how should you live your life in the coming days? Are you prepared to make the necessary sacrifices to be on mission with God? Are you prepared to walk with God at a level you never have before? If you are, then take action today. Diligently follow through with everything God has already told you to do. As you follow Jesus to be on mission in the marketplace and around the world, you will be amazed at how God uses your life to bless people everywhere you go.